LONG-RANGE INTERPRETIVE PLAN

TALLGRASS PRAIRIE
NATIONAL PRESERVE

2005

Prepared by

Department of the Interior
National Park Service

Tallgrass Prairie
National Preserve

Harpers Ferry Center
Interpretive Planning

TABLE OF CONTENTS

INTRODUCTION

Tallgrass Prairie National Preserve (TAPR) was authorized as a unit of the National Park Service in 1996 by Public Law 104-333. In December of 2000 TAPR completed its general management plan (GMP). This long-range interpretive plan will provide strategic planning for implementing the GMP's recommendations for interpretation and visitor services.

In 1995 the National Park Service issued a completely revised and updated interpretive planning chapter of the Service's Interpretation and Visitor Services Guideline, Director's Order 6 (DO-6). This revised guideline outlined the components of the Comprehensive Interpretive Plan (CIP)—a park's strategic planning document for interpretation and visitor services. Every park has been encouraged to update their interpretive planning documents using the CIP guideline. A key component of this comprehensive interpretive planning process is a long-range interpretive plan.

The long-range interpretive plan examines a park's purposes and significant resources in order to establish the park's primary interpretive themes and visitor experience goals. The plan further provides opportunities for visitors to make their own intellectual and emotional connections to the meanings and significance of the preserve's resources. The plan analyzes the park's current interpretive facilities and outlines any changes necessary to facilitate appropriate visitor experiences. The long-range interpretive plan is a concept plan that lays the groundwork for subsequent media planning and design and personal services program development. The actions recommended in the plan are those that the park can reasonably be expected to accomplish in 5 -10 years, the projected life span of a long-range interpretive plan.

BACKGROUND FOR PLANNING

Photo courtesy of Colorado Historical Society, Circa 1900

PARK PURPOSE

Park purpose is the reason or reasons for which a park area was established. These purpose statements summarize the reasons why Tallgrass Prairie National Preserve was established. They are based on the preserve's enabling legislation and legislative history. Purpose statements are important to planning because they are basic to all other assumptions about the preserve and the ways in which it should be used and managed.

The purpose of Tallgrass Prairie National Preserve is:

- to preserve, protect, and interpret for the public, an example of a tallgrass prairie ecosystem;

- to preserve and protect the cultural resources found within the preserve;

- to interpret for the public, the cultural resources and the social and cultural values represented within the preserve.

PARK SIGNIFICANCE

The significance of a park is summarized in statements that capture the essence of the park's importance to our natural and cultural heritage. Significance statements are not the same as an inventory of significant resources. While the resource inventory can be the basis on which significance is determined, the significance statements describe the importance or distinctiveness of the aggregate of resources in a park. Knowing the park's significance helps set resource protection priorities, identify primary park interpretive themes, and to develop desirable visitor experience opportunities.

The following statements of significance describe the distinctive values of Tallgrass Prairie National Preserve's resources, why these values are important within a national context, and why they contribute to the preserve's purpose.

The significance statements for Tallgrass Prairie National Preserve are:

- Of the 400,000 square miles (1,036,279 square kilometers) of tallgrass prairie ecosystem that once covered North America, less than four percent remains; Tallgrass Prairie National Preserve represents a portion of this remnant.

- The landscape of Tallgrass Prairie National Preserve contains a unique collection of natural and cultural features that tells the story of human interaction with the prairie environment from pre-European contact to the present. Some natural and cultural features consist of American Indian usages of flint from the Flint Hills and their dependency on the bison for daily survival. Cultural remnants of rock walls and foundations denote early settlement in Kansas, and water resources consisting of natural springs, seeps, and streams reflect the need for water by all cultures.

- The Spring Hill Ranch is an outstanding representation of the transition from the open range to the enclosed holdings of the large cattle companies of the 1880s.

- The Spring Hill Ranch Headquarters area contains outstanding examples of Second Empire and other 19th century architectural styles. Second Empire features are found in the main ranch house with Mansard roofs, dormer windows, molded cornices, and decorative brackets under the eaves. The ranch house also displays a rectangular tower in the front and center. Buildings that are tucked into the hills reflect an intelligent use of natural resources such as the application of sod roofs and skylights for natural insulation and cooling. Barrel-vaulted ceilings for strength and support can be seen in the root cellar, spring room, and tunnel area.

- Tallgrass Prairie National Preserve offers opportunities for extraordinary and inspirational scenic views of the Flint Hills prairie landscape.

PARK MISSION

Together, significance and purpose statements are the park's mission. The mission statement is a distillation of significance and purpose into a single statement of worth—why the park exists, what it accomplishes, and what value it offers the American people.

The mission statement for Tallgrass Prairie National Preserve is:

Tallgrass Prairie National Preserve is a public/private partnership dedicated to preserving and enhancing a nationally significant remnant of the tallgrass prairie ecosystem and the processes that sustain it; preserving and interpreting the cultural resources of the preserve and the heritage associated with the ranch property; and offering opportunities for education, inspiration, and enjoyment through public access to its geological, ecological, scenic, and historical features.

INTERPRETIVE THEMES

Interpretive themes are based on a park's purposes, significance, and primary resources. These themes are often described as the key stories or concepts that visitors should consider during and after visiting the park. The themes provide the foundation for all interpretive programs and media developed for the park. They do not include everything the park may interpret, but they do cover those ideas that are critical to visitors' understanding, appreciation, and personal connection to the park's significant resources.

The interpretive themes for Tallgrass Prairie National Preserve are:

Theme 1.

The once vast tallgrass prairie ecosystem, endemic to North America, is one of the world's most endangered ecosystems.

The critical story elements are:

- earth history prior to the last ice age
- threats to the tallgrass prairie ecosystems—both local and global
- location of the tallgrass prairie before and after human development
- maps of the tallgrass prairie ecosystem
- other locations where the tallgrass prairie exists
- nature of the tallgrass prairie; its various species and associations
- evolution of the tallgrass prairie after the ice age
- actions by people to preserve and rehabilitate the tallgrass prairie
- size of a prairie sufficient to maintain its ecosystem
- human relationship to the tallgrass prairie
- invasive species
- influence of management on prairie
- ecosystem dynamics—resilient/fragile
- long association that humans have had with this tallgrass prairie ecosystem

Interpretive objectives for this theme are:

- visitors understand the importance of the tallgrass prairie to food production
- visitors understand the significant value of the tallgrass prairie to several cultural groups
- visitors appreciate the aesthetics of the the tallgrass prairie—the space, views, and patterns

- visitors understand how the loss of heritage resources affects how we see ourselves

- visitors experience the tallgrass prairie landscape and resources

- visitors appreciate the value of diverse species to the future health of the environment

- visitors understand the value of the preserve in relation to past agricultural practices

Resources and sites related to this theme:

- ridges and high points—view of the grandeur of the horizon

- quarries (flint and limestone)

- buildings and the materials used for their construction

- bottomland along the creeks, especially after restoration; story of the threatened bottomland prairie

- interaction between the tallgrass prairie flora and fauna used in beef production

- scale and intimacy of walking on the tallgrass prairie

- burn areas

- eroding banks showing the root systems

Theme 2.

Tallgrass prairie is a biologically diverse association of flora and fauna, specially adapted over thousands of years to topography, soils, climate, fire, grazing, and other natural influences that comprise and sustain natural communities to provide an important storehouse of genetic diversity that preserves the Flint Hills prairie.

The critical story elements are:

- story of fire and the tallgrass prairie; current and historic fire regime; importance of a mosaic landscape

- topography

- relationship between soils, geology, and the tallgrass prairie
- climate—temperature, rainfall, wind—and its relationship to the tallgrass prairie
- soil and the process of building of the soils
- relationship/associations of plants and animals identified with the tallgrass prairie
- evolutionary processes at work in the tallgrass prairie
- biological reactions to restoration—bison, birds, and plants
- reaction of the tallgrass prairie to disturbance
- drought cycles and their impacts on the tallgrass prairie
- similarities and differences between various grazing animals and grazing systems
- importance of grazing to the sustainability of the tallgrass prairie; the degree of grazing pressure affects the biodiversity of the tallgrass prairie
- dynamic nature of the tallgrass prairie ecosystem, not a fixed, static system
- understanding that the tallgrass prairie is much more than "tall grass"
- guild structure where a group of plants have a similar habit of growth and nutrition
- invasive species and the cultures that brought them

Interpretive objectives for this theme are:

- visitors appreciate the beauty and biodiversity of the tallgrass prairie and the Flint Hills
- visitors understand the economic value of the tallgrass prairie biodiversity
- visitors understand the social value of the tallgrass prairie - medical potential of plants
- visitors can discuss the value of ecological diversity to humans
- visitors appreciate heritage values of the tallgrass prairie
- visitors understand the value of sustainability for humans and nature

- visitors understand the tallgrass prairie's role as an environmental health barometer—global and regional

Resources and sites related to this theme:

- bottomland areas
- ridgetops—vistas, organisms, soils, geology
- presence or absence of prairie flora
- presence or absence of prairie fauna – birds, reptiles, amphibian, mammals, and insects
- riparian areas
- burn areas
- demonstration plots
- area behind the ranch house that shows what happens in the absence of fire
- grazing areas—the associated grazers; mowing in lieu of grazers

Theme 3.

Interrelationships between the natural and cultural resources and features of the preserve reflect the influence of the land on the people and the people on the land.

The critical story elements are:

- continuum of cattle ranching and cattle management
- native peoples' use of the land and resources, i.e., bison, plants
- story of fences (keeping in and keeping out)
- consolidation of small tracts into larger ranches
- resident/non-resident ownership of ranches
- 1867 Kansas legislature ends the open range
- historic Kansa, Osage, and Wichita peoples and cultures

- prehistoric American Indian peoples and cultures

- stone technologies

- different value systems various cultures have brought to the land

- cowboy or ranching lifestyle and changes through technology

- railroad development and operation

- plow and its impact on the tallgrass prairie

- relationship between cultures, their settlement patterns, and water resources of the tallgrass prairie

- human ability to manipulate their environments

- post-depression era government erosion controls programs

- tallgrass prairie ecosystem preservation efforts

- threats to the tallgrass prairie landscape by modern human development

- gas and mineral development

- concept of the "Great American Desert" and resulting water and settlement policy

Interpretive objectives for this theme are:

- visitors understand how people interact with landscape and how landscape impacts human culture

- visitors understand the impacts human decisions have on the land even as humans depend on the land and resources

- visitors better understand the source of their food and the efforts and impacts of producing it

- visitors understand how agriculture sustainability is dependent on diversity

- visitors understand why and how the tallgrass prairie supports cattle ranching

- visitors appreciate prairie cultural heritage as an important part of American history

Resources and sites related to this theme:

- railroad spur and the shipping pens
- ranch structures
- fences
- water developments—stock ponds, springs
- flint quarries and flint working areas
- Osage orange plantings and corrals
- schoolhouse
- limestone quarries
- gas wells
- roads, trails, bridges
- archeological resources
- archival collection and objects – papers, maps, photos, furnishings, and equipment
- cattle and cattle-related structures, machinery, and ponds
- ethnographic resources—plants, flint, American Indian stories
- prairie and human interaction on the land
- Lantry house and outbuildings

Theme 4.

The cultural resources and features of the site illustrate the continuum of human experience in the Flint Hills region of Kansas from the first inhabitants through today's residents.

The critical story elements are:

- continuum of cattle ranching, management, and associated culture
- use of the land and resources by native people, e.g. bison and plants
- story of fences (in and out)

- consolidation of small tracts into larger ranches
- resident/non-resident ownership of ranches
- 1867 Kansas legislature ends the open range
- historic Kansa, Osage, and Wichita peoples and cultures
- prehistoric American Indian peoples and cultures
- stone technologies
- different value systems various cultures have brought to the land
- railroad development and operation
- plow and its impact on the tallgrass prairie
- relationship between cultures, their settlement patterns, and water resources of the tallgrass prairie
- human ability to manipulate their environments
- post-depression era government erosion control programs
- tallgrass prairie ecosystem preservation efforts
- modern human development (intrusions) threats to the tallgrass prairie landscape
- gas and mineral development
- concept of the "Great American Desert" and the resulting water and settlement policy
- evolution of human economics on the tallgrass prairie
- rise and fall of human populations on the tallgrass prairie
- displacement of cultures on this land over time
- changes in cattle and cattle management over time
- diversity of animals on the ranch
- perspectives of all the people involved in ranching
- wind power on the ranch

Interpretive objectives for this theme are:

- visitors understand how people interact with landscapes and how landscapes impact human culture

- visitors understand the impacts human decisions have on the land even as humans depend on the land and resources
- visitors better appreciate the source of their food and the efforts and impacts of producing it
- visitors understand how agricultural sustainability is dependent on diversity
- visitors understand why and how the tallgrass prairie supports cattle ranching
- visitors appreciate prairie cultural heritage as an important part of American history

Resources and sites related to this theme:

- railroad spur and the shipping pens
- ranch structures
- fences
- water developments—stock ponds, springs
- flint quarries and flint working areas
- Osage orange plantings and corrals
- schoolhouse
- limestone quarries
- gas wells
- roads, trails, bridges
- archeological resources
- cattle and cattle-related structures, machinery, and ponds
- ethnographic resources—plants, flint, American Indian stories
- archival collection and objects – papers, maps, photos, furnishings, and equipment
- Lantry house and outbuildings

Theme 5.

Tallgrass Prairie National Preserve is a new model of public/private partnership for the stewardship of resources and for providing opportunities for public enjoyment.

The critical story elements are:

- story of the development of the preserve
- controversy surrounding the development of the preserve
- roles for each public and private partner
- land ownership/lease arrangements
- park is a large public space, quite rare in Kansas
- nonprofit landowner, currently the Nature Conservancy
- many levels of partnership necessary to make the park successful

Interpretive objectives for this theme are:

- visitors understand how cooperation between public and private organizations can leverage combined resources to create a whole that is more effective than its parts
- visitors recognize that public and private funds pay to operate the preserve
- visitors understand that the preserve is composed of public and private property
- visitors understand that the success of heritage resource preservation is the responsibility of government and private sectors

Resources and sites related to this theme:

- preserved resources
- restored resources
- visitor facilities
- existence of the park

MANAGEMENT GOALS

Tallgrass Prairie National Preserve was established November 12, 1996, as a unit of the National Park System. The purpose of this unit is to preserve, protect, and interpret for the public a remnant of the once vast tallgrass prairie ecosystem. This remnant exists today because of a complex history of interaction between people and the land. The *General Management Plan / Environmental Impact Statement* for Tallgrass Prairie National Preserve puts forth a set of desired futures in order to achieve the purpose of the preserve, while reflecting its long history of interaction between people and nature. The following goals will help accomplish the vision of the preserve.

The preserve's private landowner and the National Park Service maintain a strong partnership to accomplish the mission of the preserve.

This is the primary key to success at Tallgrass Prairie National Preserve. Because ninety-eight percent of the land will remain in private ownership, the maintenance of this partnership between the landowner and the land manager is vital to the success of the preserve.

The preserve's management team maintains effective working relationships with preserve neighbors, adjacent communities, and other partners in order to identify and cooperate on issues of mutual interest.

Many issues, such as viewsheds, water quality, transportation, and fire management, can be addressed effectively only through partnership efforts; educators and researchers may have important current knowledge, other landowners may have similar needs and concerns; nearby communities may have additional valuable resources. Accommodating diverse viewpoints and interests, and sharing information, will be very important for the successful, long-term management of the preserve.

The preserve has adequate information available for making management decisions.

There is a need to establish a long-term inventory and monitoring program at the preserve. The current state of the resources of the preserve must be established as baseline data. Then, quantitative and qualitative changes must be identified over time. Only through a comprehensive inventory and monitoring program can adequate information be made available for sound decision making.

Management activities and policies at the preserve lead to the enhancement of the tallgrass prairie ecosystem and a greater understanding of its associated processes.

Experts have consistently stated that to enhance the tallgrass prairie ecosystem it is important to maintain the processes that allow for its full expression; it is less important to focus only on increasing the number of species present. The preserve provides opportunities at the local, regional, and national level to demonstrate and create a better understanding of these processes.

Heterogeneous disturbance regimes are an integral part of management activities at the preserve.

Experts suggest that in order to allow for the full expression of the tallgrass prairie ecosystem, elements of randomness should be encouraged. The complex interrelationships found within the prairie ecosystem, especially those involving fire and grazing, should be perpetuated in such a way as to ensure that the same activity (such as fire or grazing) does not occur in the same area, in the same way, at the same time, every year.

The preserve's seeps, springs, and streams remain in good ecological condition and support a healthy and diverse aquatic community.

Healthy aquatic resources are vital to a fully functioning prairie ecosystem. These resources should be assessed and either maintained or restored to function as integral parts of the ecosystem.

Open and unobstructed views, an integral part of the prairie experience, are maintained.

The vistas and views have been repeatedly identified by the public as some of the preserve's most important resources. The relationship of earth and sky, the feeling of vastness (during both day and night), and the openness of the landscape all contribute to a "sense of place." Existing developments should be managed to enhance views (e.g., bury power lines), and future developments should enhance and not detract from this important resource.

Resources are managed to interpret the legacy of human interaction in the Flint Hills.

The tallgrass prairie has evolved through the complex interplay between climate, geology, grazing, fire, and human activities. The span and variety of human activities in the Flint Hills appear to be well represented at the preserve. These stories should be told in large part through and by the resources of the preserve.

Natural and cultural resources are managed to preserve the character-defining features of the Flint Hills cultural landscape.

The Flint Hills landscape today represents the dynamic inter-relationship of people and the land. Maintenance and enhancement of the tallgrass prairie ecosystem should be done in such a way that this landscape is maintained.

The preserve's historic records and objects are properly managed and preserved.

Historic records and objects should be an integral part of education and interpretation programming at the preserve. Preservation and use of these materials can bring visitors into direct contact with the story of the preserve. Archive materials should be available to researchers.

Education and interpretation efforts extend beyond the boundary of the preserve in order to reach a wide audience.

Although on-site experiences will be a very important part of education and interpretation at the preserve, interpretive efforts cannot be successful if they are directed only toward those who visit a site. Outreach to communities, educational institutions, and potential visitors through off-site activities, dissemination of written materials, and development of long-distance learning opportunities should be pursued.

Visitors are transported to and through the preserve using a variety of transportation modes, in order to protect the landscape and provide for high-quality visitor experiences.

Because of the desire to preserve the landscape and protect integral parts of the prairie experience, a transportation system other than personal automobiles might be needed. The system could transport visitors from a visitor center to the historic ranch headquarters area or from one visitor area to another. A range of alternative visitor transportation modes will need to be considered. These options could closely tie transportation to interpretation, and should address safety issues, including potential conflicts between grazers and visitors.

THE VISITORS

Between 1998 and 2004, Tallgrass Prairie National Preserve averaged 17,584 visitors a year. Visitation has been relatively consistent most of the year (April-November) with the months December through March as the off-season (illustrated in the following table and chart).

MONTH/ YEAR	VISITATION 1998-2004						
	1998	1999	2000	2001	2002	2003	2004
January	172	281	365	328	365	325	241
February	332	734	434	330	377	389	306
March	387	979	953	962	994	675	671
April	1,587	1,331	1,336	1,624	1,084	1,063	1,225
May	3,045	3,120	2,631	2,615	2,307	2,861	2,450
June	2,640	3,355	2,925	2,756	2,473	2,391	2,160
July	2,988	2,446	2,301	1,767	1,819	1,695	2,080
August	2,230	2,210	1,494	1,574	1,509	1,364	1,407
September	2,035	2,099	1,834	1,955	2,090	1,763	1,874
October	2,192	2,797	1,916	2,536	1,754	2,332	1,928
November	1,041	1,746	723	1,084	1,169	629	623
December	345	402	229	443	458	309	316
Total	18,994	21,500	17,141	17,974	16,399	15,796	15,281

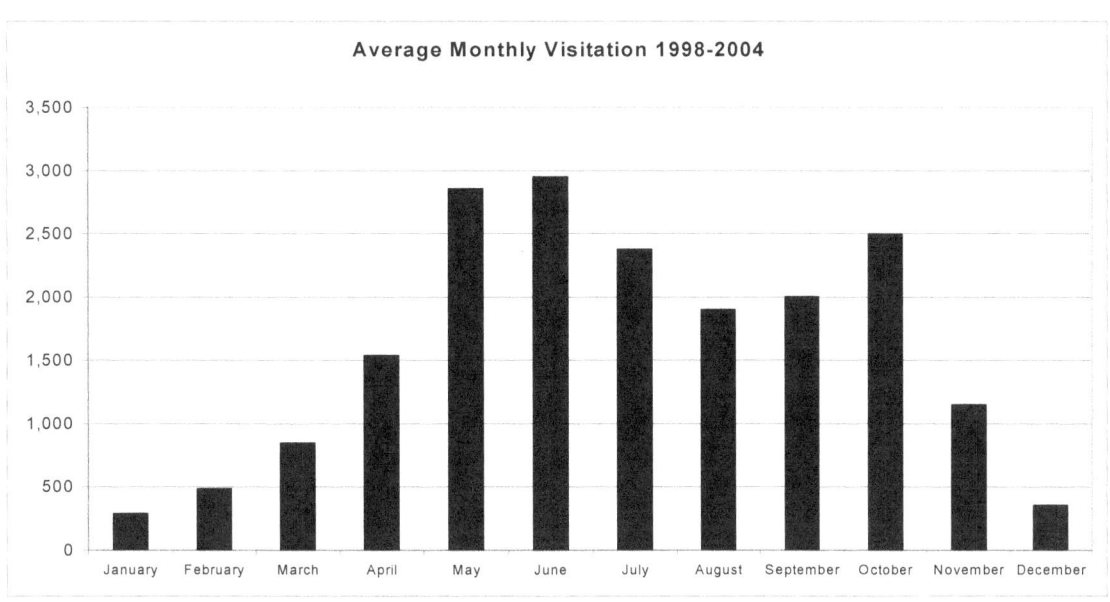

Since Tallgrass Prairie National Preserve is a new national park area, no formal studies of its visitors have been completed. The information that follows was collected by knowledgeable professionals who conducted a year-long visitor demographics survey by observing visitors and utilizing information from the visitor sign-in sheets. These bullet statements provide insight into the audiences and potential audiences for interpretive and visitor services.

- Older population—27% of the visitors are over 60

- 30 -60 years old—48% of total visitation

- teenagers/young adults—13% of total visitation

- under 14 years old – 12% of total visitation

- 93% of visitors come in groups of 2 or more

- 7 % of visitors come alone

- 61% of visitors are from within the state of Kansas

- 26% of visitors come from the rest of the United States

- 11% of visitors come from the region – Nebraska, Oklahoma, Colorado, Missouri

- 2 % of visitors are international

- 5% of visitors come in organized groups
- School children—education groups, mostly come in April and May—5% of total visitation
- average visitor stay is one hour and thirty minutes
- current facilities could handle 30 -40,000 visitors per year
- 98% of the visitors are white
- visitors are curious about "tall grass," the house, the barn
- visitors want to show younger people how things used to be
- nature lovers want to watch birds and hike into the prairie
- visitors come to learn about natural and cultural features
- visitors come to have an educational experience
- visitors come for the views
- visitors come to participate in available resource appropriate recreational opportunities, e.g. picnicking, bird watching, hiking, and tours.
- visitors come because it is a National Park Service site
- visitors enjoy the tours—prairie/house
- visitors want to see what the focus of the park establishment controversy was about
- stop on the scenic byway
- scout activities
- American Indians may want to participate in cultural activities
- visitors want to see tall grass
- if available, people would probably enjoy seeing bison, hiking, primitive camping, backpacking, and trail riding

VISITOR EXPERIENCE GOALS

Visitor experience goals are statements that describe those fundamental visitor experience opportunities which Tallgrass Prairie National Preserve, through its visitor services and interpretive program, wants most to facilitate. Visitors cannot be required to have certain experiences, but the preserve has identified important experiences that should be available to them. In planning facilities, interpretive media, and personal services, Tallgrass Prairie National Preserve will work to create and enhance opportunities for these experiences.

Visitors will have opportunities to:

- understand the role of partnerships at the preserve
- become emotionally involved with the prairie through a variety of media
- create a sense of stewardship for the tallgrass prairie
- experience the resources in solitude and through social or structured activities
- experience the tallgrass prairie through direct contact
- appreciate the expanse of the tallgrass prairie through unimpeded views of the Flint Hills landscape

- gain a sense of some of the daily and annual activities of the people who have lived here and continue to live here

- appreciate cultural landscapes, structures, and artifacts representative of various periods of habitation at the preserve

- experience and understand indigenous prairie plants and animals, and the processes through which they are interrelated

- understand the interrelationships between people and the landscape

- experience the natural restoration processes of the prairie and appreciate the prairie's resiliency

- experience universally accessible facilities and programs where feasible

- experience a variety of recreational activities that are appropriate, feasible, and do not impact critical resources

- appreciate the "prairie underground" as the non-visible element of the ecosystem

- be moved to personal action toward the protection of prairie and other natural and cultural landscapes

- appreciate the role of fire and grazing in the prairie ecosystem

- experience a greater personal "sense of place"

- appreciate the role of springs, seeps, streams, and other riparian areas as a part of the prairie

- understand key prairie ecological processes and relationships

- appreciate the special experiences of prairie sights, sounds, skyscapes, views, and feelings during all seasons and times—and during both day and night

- participate in ranch activities and farming through cultural demonstrations

- participate in American Indian cultural activities

- leave with the further desire to explore the prairie and share the desire with others

- identify and learn about different prairie organisms

- experience a variety of recreational activities where appropriate, feasible, and where those activities don't impact critical resources

- experience the night sky

Front of the Lower Fox Creek Schoolhouse lit by the glow of a controlled burn.

ISSUES AND INFLUENCES

The following is a list of items which have an impact on the Tallgrass Prairie National Preserve's abilities to reach its interpretive and visitor experience goals.

- A general management plan will guide the development of the preserve.

- The vast majority of the preserve property is under a 35-year cattle lease. The lessee manages fire and grazing differently than envisioned by the preserve's general management plan.

- The preserve property is under a 35-year oil and gas lease.

- Drought affects what visitors see and creates added fire potential.

- Safety issues related to weather, fire, cattle, and bison can impact recreational use.

- The preserve has many research needs—prairie, biotic monitoring, and archeology; research activities may temporarily constrain visitor activities.

- All development decisions on private preserve property require the consent and involvement of the landowner.

- Adjacent landowners have concern about bison, fire management, and fencing; the preserve has concerns about the land uses of its neighbors.

- Bison and bison management will attract visitors, but may also constrain other experiences, such as hiking.

- Facility and program development must follow appropriate compliance procedures.

- Funding and funding cycles impact all management and operational activities.

- If the preserve does not acquire historic ranch machinery and tools, it may limit the effectiveness of interpretation and the recreation of the historic scene.

- The difficulty in acquiring readily available stock that meets stringent guidelines could slow the progress of development.

- Incomplete plans or the lack of plans will affect the development of the interpretive program.

- Possible land easement issues may be an issue for the preserve.

- Highway conditions such as high speed traffic, limited sight lines, and rights-of-way create safety concerns for visitors and employees.

- A shuttle system may or may not be established.

- Private sector development of campgrounds may have an influence on the park.

- The privately owned Lantry house is a bed and breakfast. Three other Lantry outbuildings are currently owned by the private partner. The property is not planned for visitor use.

- Strong City sewage treatment plant is visible near the south boundary.

- The small staff, mostly seasonal and temporary employees, faces many competing interests for time.

- The preserve has no formal museum collection nor does it have a collection management plan.

- The preserve needs historic furnishing reports.

- There is a need to reuse a structure for restrooms at the ranch.

- A limited number of oral histories are available, but there is a lot more potential for additional work.

- Matfield Green, Konza, Ordway Prairie groups are making efforts in curriculum-based education.

- There is a need for ethnographic studies.

- There is a need for more research on settlement and ranching heritage—both in the Flint Hills and at the Spring Hill / Z Bar Ranch.

- There is a need for more American Indian cultural information.

EXISTING CONDITIONS

- The historic ranch headquarters area is open year-round 9 a.m. to 4:30 p.m., except Thanksgiving, Christmas, and New Years Days. There is a self-guided brochure for the area.

- The bookstore is operated by the Kansas Park Trust. National Park Service staff helps operate the bookstore during the winter months.

- House tours are conducted hourly from 9:30 a.m. to 3:30 p.m. from the last weekend in April through the last weekend in October. House tours are available during November through March on an as needed basis.

- Two self-guiding interpretive trails, the Southwind Nature Trail and Bottomland Trail, are open daily during daylight hours.

- Three backcountry day hiking trails are open from 9:00 a.m. to 3:30 p.m. with a free hiking permit. A hiking brochure with map has been developed for these new backcountry day hiking trails.

- The Lower Fox Creek School is staffed by volunteers and is only open on weekends in May, June, September, and October.

- Bus tours begin the last weekend in April and run through the last weekend in October. They are available daily at 11 a.m., 1 p.m., and 3 p.m. Cost: $5.00 adult, $3.00 age 5-18 years, and free age 4 and under.

- Group tours (for groups of 15 or more) of the historic ranch headquarters and/or the prairie are available by reservation with two weeks advance notice. Ranch headquarters tour is $4.00 per adult, $2.00 age 5 – 18 years, and 4 and under is free. Combination ranch headquarters and prairie bus tour is $7.00 per adult, $4.00 age 5-18, and 4 and under are free.

- School groups (second grade through high school) accommodated by reservation and a $1.00 fee per student. The current educational program is not curriculum-based except for a curriculum-based educational program at the Lower Fox Creek School where 2nd through 4th grade children experience a school day in the 19th century. Children dress in period costume, walk to and from school through the prairie, eat a cold lunch, and experience lessons that were appropriate for their age level during the 19th century.

- The preserve operates a visitor contact station/information desk in the barn from May through October.

- The preserve operates a visitor contact station/information desk on the back porch of the ranch house from November through April.

- The preserve presents a number of off-site programs; some explain the preserve's planning processes and provide general park information, while other programs offer specific natural and cultural subjects.

- The preserve has developed a partnership with local scouts to do trail work and other maintenance functions as needed.

- The preserve has developed a living history interpretive program on weekends from Memorial Day weekend through the last weekend of October. Programs interpret ranching legacy themes.

- The park's brochure was originally produced by the National Park Trust. It included an activity/program insert that has been developed and produced by the National Park Service following the guidelines of the NPS Graphic Identity Program. A new color brochure has been developed for the preserve that explains the preserve partners and available activities. The brochure has been translated into Spanish.

- There is a self-guided brochure for the ranch headquarters area and Southwind Nature Trail and another brochure for the Bottomland Trail.

- A Junior Ranger booklet (both color and black/white) has been developed for visiting children.

- The preserve has a park website. The address is www.nps.gov/tapr.

- The preserve offers an updated 10-minute audiovisual program with closed captioning.

- A bird list brochure has been developed using the NPS Graphic Identity Program.

- There is a geology site bulletin using the new standards.

- A plant list brochure has been developed using the new standards.

- In the ranch headquarters and overlook area there are 14 wayside exhibits and kiosks.

Other sites that interpret or share Tallgrass Prairie National Preserve themes:

- the Flint Hills Scenic Byway

- Cottonwood Falls courthouse and jail tours

- Roniger Museum

- Chase County Historical Society

- Konza Prairie Biological Station

- Council Grove-10 historical sites related to the Santa Fe Trail

- Council Grove Lake - nature trail

- Little John Creek Reserve

- Maxwell Game Preserve

- Ordway Prairie Preserve

- Flint Hills Preserve-not open to the public

- Tallgrass Prairie Preserve in Oklahoma

- Overland Wagon Train

- Fort Riley

- Great Plains Nature Center—Wichita

- Milford Nature Center

- Kanza Museum—Oklahoma

- Agricultural Hall of Fame

- Emporia State University Geology Museum

- Kansas State Historical Society

- Natural History Museum at Kansas University
- Emporia State University one-room schoolhouse
- Kansas State University range management program

FUTURE PROGRAM DESCRIPTION

OUTREACH

Visitor Experience Prescription – GMP

The National Park Service would actively seek partnerships and opportunities for cooperation with local communities, government agencies, nonprofit organizations, and other entities that may have an interest in helping achieve the preserve's desired future conditions. The National Park Service also would cooperate and partner to help others achieve their goals outside the preserve when such cooperation would also advance a purpose for which the preserve was created.

Recommendations

Continue to update and expand the preserve's Internet website. The depth and breadth of current content is excellent with extensive, up-to-date interpretive text and well-chosen photos. As the preserve's development continues, redesign of the web site will make navigation from page to page easier and improve visual consistency with an overall thematic appearance. A preserve employee or contracted web coordinator will update and maintain the site with advancing technology. Updated topics will include prairie restoration, Junior Ranger program, QuickTime Virtual Reality (VR) 360-degree views of the prairie at different times of the year, and educational activities for teachers and children.

Develop, coordinate and present personal service programs to nearby communities. Interpretive, educational, and informational activities will encourage stakeholder participation and support of preserve programs. Managers will encourage all preserve staff to participate in activities sponsored by organizations that foster communication, recognition, and acceptance of the preserve and its programs. Preserve staff will take personal service programs to local people who may not visit the preserve. Activities will help neighbors understand management and staff actions, provide basic understanding of preserve activities and values, and alleviate misconceptions about the preserve.

Revise preserve highway sign plan to improve way-finding. The distance of the preserve from major travel routes requires an expanded sign program to improve navigation from major highways and nearby cities. Preserve and Kansas transportation agency staffs will explore sign improvements along U.S. Highway 50, Kansas State Highway 177(Flint Hills Scenic Byway), Interstates 35, 335, and 70 to provide clear, accurate, and convenient way-finding. Signs should include a clearly identifiable visual image, such as the National Park Service arrowhead, for easy recognition from fast moving vehicles.

Use existing Kansas State Highway 177 (Flint Hills Scenic Byway) to develop a connection between the preserve and Santa Fe Trail at Council Grove. A scenic/historic route could be interpreted to capture travelers and direct them to the preserve. An interpretive exhibit at Council Grove and information exhibit at the preserve might be linked with a motor tour guide to interpret the tallgrass prairie ecosystem and the Flint Hills ranching culture.

Plan and develop traveling exhibits. Moveable wayside exhibits, portable museum exhibits employing concepts described in section "Preserve-Wide Recommendations – Exhibits" of this plan, or a Harpers Ferry Center Discovery Station are appropriate for a variety of audiences and display sites. Traveling exhibits can accommodate education curricula geared toward school groups or exhibits reflecting seasonal changes in the prairie or in ranch operations.

Continue development and marketing of the Traveling Trunk Program. Preserve staff and partners will plan and produce ten interpretive and educational activity packets for on-site and off-site use. Trunks will explore the many subjects related to the preserve's five interpretive themes. Each trunk will contain a variety of media accompanied by activity sheets and objects appropriate to the theme of the trunk. All trunks will include curriculum-based activities for different grade levels.

Focus some outreach activities to specific stakeholder populations near the preserve. Activities can be targeted to large regional populations, such as ranching and Hispanic/Latino cultures or culturally affiliated tribes. Information can be distributed through Spanish language and ranching publications and radio. Interpretation can link cattle ranching in the United States and Mexico. Interpretive staff will present stories of Hispanic ranchers and cowboys that pertain to the Flint Hills and can be supported by documented research. Other ethnic contributions concerning ranching and uses of the land will be researched and presented as appropriate.

PRESERVE-WIDE RECOMMENDATIONS

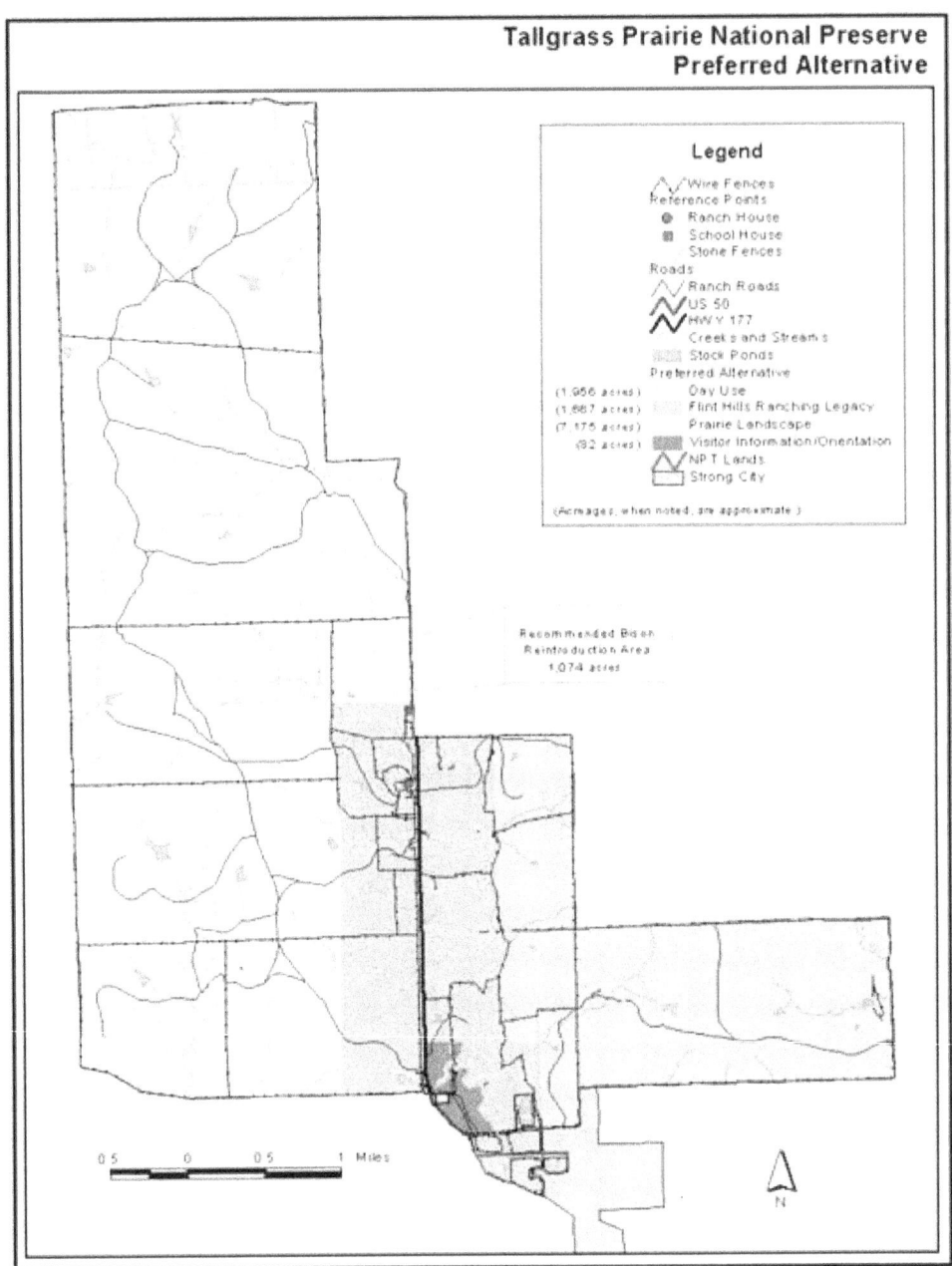

Visitor Experience Prescription – GMP

Integrated management of natural and cultural resources will reflect the intertwining of resources. Management of natural resources will focus on ecological, educational, and inspirational values of the tallgrass prairie and on understanding and facilitating processes that permit the prairie to express itself. Many cultural resources are clustered in sites or complexes that represent more than one historic period and have associations with several themes. A historic structures report, cultural landscape report, and other studies and plans will guide management decisions and help determine the focus of cultural resource interpretation.

A variety of visitor activities and facilities appropriate for a national preserve will respond to diverse visitor interests, time commitments, and levels of physical exertion. Onsite interpretive and educational programs will focus on natural history of the tallgrass prairie, Flint Hills ranching legacy, and the history and culture of American Indians.

Recommendations

General

The preserve will establish geographic interpretation areas that reflect the distinctive character of different sections of the preserve. Based on key resource features and visitor experience opportunities the preserve has been divided by the general management plan into four management areas: Visitor Information and Orientation, Flint Hills Ranching Legacy, Day Use, and Prairie Landscape. This will diversify use by providing visitors a variety of opportunities to experience all management areas. This long-range interpretive plan will further divide those management areas into geographic interpretive areas: Outreach, Preserve-Wide Recommendations, Ranch Headquarters Complex, Lower Fox Creek School, Bottomland Prairie, Upland Prairie, Day Use Area, and Visitor Center.

Develop interpretation and education activities that reflect the dynamics and diversity of the tallgrass prairie ecosystem. Visitor experience opportunities will emphasize the diversity of the prairie and the natural resource management activities to restore and maintain an environment where a cubic meter of the tallgrass prairie may contain a diversity of 40 various species. Visitors who travel to the preserve in different seasons and years can see a varied environment.

Develop interpretation that integrates natural and cultural resources. The preserve presents an exciting and unusual balance of natural and cultural resources. The dominating human-made structures at the ranch headquarters complex tend to create an impression that the purpose of the preserve focuses on the story of ranching. Visitors might ask, where is the tallgrass promised in the preserve's name? Interpretation needs to integrate and balance the five interpretive themes. Interpreting a "Living in the Tallgrass" concept could emphasize natural and cultural stories. This concept can apply to the cultural history of American Indians, settlers, ranchers, and present day residents and visitors as well as the natural history of plant and animal adaptations to the area.

Interpretive media will be designed and positioned to be as inconspicuous as possible. In the effort to interpret the various features of this preserve it is important that chosen media devices are appropriate to the function they serve. Devices used, such as wayside exhibits, informational signs, commemorative plaques, and outdoor exhibits, must not impose themselves to the detriment of the cultural landscape and historic structures they interpret.

Exhibits

Planning and implementation of the preserve exhibit program will be approached in two phases: pre-visitor center and post-visitor center. Prior to development of a visitor center, orientation, information, and interpretive exhibits will continue to be displayed at the ranch headquarters complex. After development of the visitor center, interpretive and orientation exhibits will be concentrated in the new center. Specific exhibit recommendations for both phases are presented in **RANCH HEADQUARTERS COMPLEX** and **VISITOR CENTER** sections of this plan.

Preserve staff will plan and produce orientation and interpretation exhibits for the barn and ranch house to serve visitors until a visitor center is developed. In the event that considerable time should pass before a visitor center is in place, interim interpretive devices will be needed for an increasing number of visitors. Interpretive devices such as site identifiers, signs, trail markers, indoor directional guides, indoor exhibits, and visual props to aid personal presentations will be produced by preserve staff utilizing skills already present. All these devices will display professional design standards following the National Park Service Graphic Identity Program.

Exhibit concepts in **APPENDICES** illustrate possible interim exhibits that can be adapted to various sites. These concepts provide temporary solutions for exhibit issues at this point in the preserve's development. The simplicity and lightness of some concepts could suggest their use for off-site visits to schools, shopping malls, fairs, airports, and other public places. Exhibits produced with these concepts can be used for front-end evaluation of exhibits proposed for the visitor center. Interim exhibits in the barn and ranch house can analyze concepts before investing in production and installation of permanent exhibits. Some exhibits produced with these concepts might even be used as part of the future visitor center exhibit area.

Design, production, and installation plans for visitor use areas to feature museum exhibits will be developed as soon as possible. Exhibits and post-visitor center activities will be developed when funding for implementation appears imminent. Plans for the barn, ranch house, and proposed visitor center will include label copy, design elements, and graphic components for new exhibits.

Historic furnishing reports for visitor use areas that will feature accurately furnished spaces will be developed as soon as possible. The reports will evaluate and validate existing furnishings. They will recommend additional furnishings to enhance historic appearances that reflect the lifestyle of historic occupants and users.

Access

The preserve will place a high priority on making existing programs and facilities accessible for all visitors. Preserve staff and consultants will periodically review activities and facilities and recommend appropriate improvements.

Design of new facilities and media will provide optimum access for visitors and employees. The Architectural Barriers Act and the American's With Disabilities Act establish standards for physical access. All new interpretive media will conform to National Park Service Programmatic Accessibility Guidelines for Interpretive Media.

Alternative interpretation methods at facilities near areas that cannot be made physically accessible will enable all visitors to

understand and appreciate the resource. Photographs on wayside exhibits and publications can bring distant, inaccessible sights to visitors at the trailhead or parking areas. Trail descriptions on all trailhead exhibits will include levels of access.

The preserve's interpretive program will provide multilingual information to an appropriate extent based on current visitation. Interpretive managers and accessibility specialists will decide the needed extent. A moderate approach will initially provide fundamental information in a few languages. The number of activities offered in Spanish will increase to address a large regional Hispanic / Latino population. Continuous assessment of visitation trends will determine the future need for multilingual information and interpretation.

Focus an element of the preserve outreach program on Hispanic / Latino population. The 2000 census demographic profile of Emporia reported that 21.5% of the population indicated that they were Hispanic/Latino. This percentage is nearly twice the 12.5% national average and higher than any major cities near the park: Kansas City 16.8%, Wichita 9.6%, and Topeka 8.9%. Tallgrass Prairie National Preserve could be at the forefront in welcoming this cultural community to national parks, while creating a strong constituency.

Design, fabricate, and install an interactive video kiosk. A kiosk displayed in an area accessible to all visitors can make less accessible areas of the barn, ranch house, and prairie visually available. Current technology can provide reasonable access for visitors without impacting the historic integrity of structures and landscapes at the ranch. A computer kiosk located in the barn or ranch house might show QuickTime Virtual Reality (VR) clips of each room in the ranch house and barn. A computer running an internal website can provide real time images. The kiosk could also present visitor information that can be easily updated with current activities, special event schedules, and safety messages. Other interpretive elements could be incorporated into the kiosk. Ranger-led guided tours could be videotaped and presented on the kiosk. Kiosk design must be compatible with the historic character of 19th century buildings.

Audiovisual

Develop new audiovisual program upon completion of the visitor center. A 10 – 15 minute film or high definition video with three channels or surround sound mix will explore the preserve and the five interpretive themes. The audiovisual program will reflect the diversity and significance of ecosystem resources. It will depict components of the ecosystem that are difficult for most visitors to see as they travel through the preserve. It can change misconceptions that tallgrass means seven foot tall grasses everywhere. The program can reflect different time periods of human use of the tallgrass prairies using preserve resources as examples. The program would also touch on the natural and cultural areas related to the five interpretive themes. Audiovisual programs will be translated into several foreign languages and shown in the visitor center theater as described in **VISITOR CENTER – Interior Spaces.**

Develop a videotape and DVD sales item. This video and DVD will be designed to be a valuable interpretive and souvenir product. It will present all the major visitor experience opportunities available at the preserve. It can include a narrated prairie bus tour, a walking tour of the ranch complex, a guided tour of the ranch house, an education program at the schoolhouse, living history in the ranch headquarters area, and a stroll along the Bottomland Trail.

Develop a CD ROM of images of the ranch and prairie for sale in the bookstore.

Create and continually augment an image reference file. The file should become an exhaustive collection of images pertaining to preserve stories. Historic photos and graphics, development drawings and diagrams, resource photos, and images of visitor activities need to be sought and organized for future use. Scanning them at appropriate specifications will make them digitally accessible and protect the hard-copy originals from frequent handling. Images from digital cameras can also be kept in this file; however, when making photographic records — whether by staff members or commissioned professionals—35mm transparencies are the standard for quality, scanning ease, and storage. Digital images are poorer and not recommended. Information relating to the photos, including model releases, ownership, and proper credits will be maintained with the reference file.

Collections Management

As a new national park area with pending permanent collections (all objects presently owned by The Nature Conservancy) there are some basic collections management steps that can be taken. These will help preserve staff determine what to acquire and ultimately will better support the preserve's interpretive program.

Acquire items in accordance with an approved Scope of Collections Statement. Artifacts, archival material, natural history collections, and oral histories collected will relate to and be directly associated with the preserve. These items will be collected, preserved and managed for use in museum exhibits, interpretive programs, and public and scholarly research.

Systematically photograph all objects at the preserve. The photographs will include all objects in storage and on display in the barn, ranch house, outbuildings, and school. The fastest, most efficient approach would be narrated video. Quality of images will not be as good as other formats but will provide visual identity in the event of damage or loss.

Contract an agricultural equipment specialist to assess farm and ranch objects. The preserve has some farm and ranch equipment with brief information about them. An assessment should include object identification, date, origins/provenance, condition, and description of function and significance. Completion of the assessment will help preserve staff determine what objects they want to acquire for museum storage or display in permanent exhibitions.

Assess ranch house artifacts to determine their origins, provenance, period of manufacture, and condition. The preserve has a good inventory of the artifacts in the Spring Hill Ranch house. An assessment of these objects will provide critical information for developing a historic furnishings report in order to determine a period of interpretation for the house and acquire items for the permanent collection.

Complete an assessment of artifacts in Lower Fox Creek School. This assessment will follow the same recommendations previously described for the barn and ranch house. It can likely be completed by the same person who assesses ranch house objects. Chase County

Historical Society has a collection of artifacts related to early schools in the area. That organization is a good resource for area history and artifacts appropriate for the schoolhouse.

Education

Continue using existing facilities and programs and develop new ones as time and funding permits. Preserve management and staff will strive to accomplish the education initiatives described in the preserve's current education program. They will develop educational activities to optimize potential opportunities this site has to offer schools. Here teachers can provide literature, writing, art, social science, history and science lessons to students. There is great potential for immersion and living history programs. The following recommendations will augment activities currently available.

The education program will fit established Kansas curricula and reflect national standards. Pre-visit activities will prepare teachers and students for an educational visit. Post-visit activities will reinforce topics discussed at the preserve to extend learning experiences throughout the school year. Time spent at the preserve will include curriculum-based activities and immersion experiences with resources.

Integration of content areas will be a prime focus for future program development. New activities developed for the education program will reflect real-life applications for compatibility with current school requirements. Preserve and school staffs must be aware of various learning styles and develop activities that respond effectively to as many styles as possible. Format of activities will provide multilevel opportunities within each activity to reach different levels of intelligence and interest universally found within school groups.

Preserve staff will explore potential distance learning opportunities. Cooperation with regional schools and national education organizations will identify current and future technologies planned to link schools to other education resources. Preserve education program managers will prepare a proposal to implement a distance learning program in partnership with area school districts. A linked education program will enable students to interact with educators and scientists via the Internet and other distance learning venues. Education program managers will revise and reprint the education plan and assess potential to redesign the program to reach a global audience.

Enhance partnerships and affiliations with colleges and universities. Preserve staff will explore opportunities to establish a cooperative program with Emporia State University, Kansas State University, and other colleges to offer student teacher internships and other training. Students participating in approved education classes at colleges or universities could spend time at the preserve honing their outdoor teaching skills.

Seek funding to establish an education specialist position at the preserve. An education specialist will coordinate the curriculum-based education program and attend faculty meetings, in-service workshops, seminars, and teacher meetings.

Establish an education advisory and implementation group to assist with program development. As a general rule, only develop education programs in conjunction with teachers. The group can provide outside perspectives to help preserve staff generate new education activity ideas. The group will include representatives of school districts, education associations, university professors, and state department of education representatives. Group members may also assist with classroom instruction and presentation of teacher workshops. Several classroom teachers will be included in the advisory group to assure that activities developed align with classroom requirements.

Implement training and internship programs for education partners. One goal of the education program will be well-educated, confident teachers who are knowledgeable of preserve themes and who can present education activities independently. That requires a change in focus from the normal goal of a well-educated student. Teacher training sponsored by the preserve will include techniques to help teachers feel comfortable in conducting learning experiences in outdoor environments at the preserve or elsewhere. One element of preserve-produced teacher training will focus on future teachers who are still in college. All new teachers participating in the education program will receive copies of activities developed by experienced teachers and successfully implemented in an outdoor setting.

Develop a funding strategy for implementing additional education programs. Education program managers will seek appropriated funds to meet current and future demands for educational services. Preserve staff will commit to find and tap varied and sustainable funding sources. Funds will enable preserve staff to maintain current programs and develop new ones. Preserve managers will create an interdisciplinary team of staff to identify cross-division education projects and funding sources for them.

Establish and maintain currency. An effective education program will require frequent curriculum refinement and constant interaction between teachers and preserve staff, so both can quickly learn of changes in program activities. Future program development will assure that activities are compatible with classroom need. Preserve education program managers will establish verbal or written teacher assessment of the program to assure adherence to current trends in education. Staff will contact Kansas Department of Education to learn the state's current testing subject and schedule of additional assessments.

Partnerships

Further develop community partnerships with local, state, and federal agencies.

Maintain intra-preserve partnerships to effectively use available National Park Service and primary landowning partner personnel. Frequent interaction between interpretation and education program personnel, staff, and managers of other disciplines at work in park management will assure that all employees are well-informed to complete their tasks. The interpretation and education function will be severely limited in its effectiveness without close coordination and mutual support of other primary preserve partners.

Continue partnership with the primary partners to provide interpretation to visitors. The partners can pursue grants to support interpretation and education and develop and distribute interpretive sales items through the preserve bookstore. Sharing space and production costs for preserve publications can provide a well-rounded range of visitor uses, activities, and interests.

Develop partnership with other prairie and ranching national park units and organizations outside the National Park System. Activities may include sharing of expertise and funding for marketing, training, historical and natural research, special events and seminars, exhibit planning and development, site promotion, tours, and other joint projects. For example, a handbook might be developed that focuses on a particular theme and features complimentary stories from several parks and areas as described in **PRESERVE-WIDE RECOMMENDATIONS** – Publications.

Interpretive division employees will explore potential to establish and maintain strong partnerships with representatives of American Indian nations and tribes. These partnerships are critical to effectively tell stories related to the preserve. Fundamental questions must be answered to cement effective, long-lasting partnerships between the preserve and American Indian stakeholders. How can the preserve better address American Indian themes and stories? Which elements of those stories can preserve staff relate to visitors and which are best told by native people? To the extent practical preserve managers will recruit from American Indian communities to participate in interpretive, educational, and information programs.

Continue to identify and market volunteer opportunities at the preserve. Enlist schools and volunteer individuals and groups to help with resource restoration activities and special events. Explore potential to develop education activities with local 4-H groups. Seek other groups interested in volunteer activities supporting education, interpretation and information programs.

Develop partnerships with professional and educational organizations. Colleges, universities, and organizations can be solicited to contract or contribute services such as historic research, professional assessments of natural and cultural resources, and collection and evaluation of visitor survey data.

Personal Services

Continue to improve current personal service activities: stationed assignments, guided walking tours, prairie bus tours, ranch house tours, and education programs. Personal service activities will continue to be a core component of the overall interpretive operation. Personal contact between the interpreter and the visitor has several advantages over most other media.

Plan and present a series of park-wide special events. Preserve staff will sponsor and/or assist with special events both on and offsite. Each event will be compatible with preserve purpose and themes. Suggested events include cultural music programs, traditional holiday decorations, harvest festival, prairie days, and night sky program.

Develop a series of programs for children. Designate special days for children to visit the preserve. Each day can be dedicated to presentation of activities related to a specific theme. Children might experience specific resources such as the prairie, the working ranch, or the schoolhouse, or they might talk to a ranger or other preserve employee to learn what working for a national park entails.

Develop components of the living history program for presentation in first person format. Preserve staff will research and document opportunities for first person interpretation. Staff and volunteers knowledgeable of preserve themes and history and trained in first person techniques will plan and present activities. Such activities might be appropriate in the ranch headquarters area and at the schoolhouse where a historic setting will allow true living history experiences. Adapt activities to costumed interpretation for presentation in areas where first person format is not appropriate.

Dedicate considerable staff time to media development until the preserve interpretive program is fully developed. National Park Service studies have shown that 60% of visitors interact with media while only 40 % go on tours. This statistic suggests that a large portion of available staff would be well used for media development. In this early stage of development the preserve has a huge interpretive media task before it to develop a park brochure, write and print several site bulletins, revise and update wayside exhibits, and create visitor center exhibits.

Develop a training program appropriate for all staff presenting information, interpretation, and education activities to the public. The training program will include components that focus on content, accuracy, completeness, and interpretive and communication skills necessary for preparing and presenting programs and activities. Interpreters' familiarity with the preserve, current research findings, interpretive methods, and evaluation techniques must be coupled with objectivity and sensitivity to controversial issues, policies, and management directives.

The personal service program will encourage and facilitate operational division cross over. Interpreters will request and use information from other division staff to present to the public in an interpretive format. Staff of other divisions and guest speakers from outside the preserve who are interested and capable can present programs to staff and the public.

Preserve interpretive manager will routinely evaluate all personal service activities and adapt as needed to assure thematic depth and diversity. Continuous appraisal will focus activities on specific resources and compelling stories and assure that visitor needs and management goals are met with the greatest possible effectiveness. Staff will regularly monitor visitor use in all areas of the preserve and develop personal service activities in response to changing visitation patterns.

Publications

Tallgrass Prairie National Preserve's publications program currently has nine national park produced publications available to the public.

Develop a publications identity based on the National Park Service Graphics Identity Program. The current publications reflect a good effort for a new national park with a small staff. Because publications are seen by every visitor to a national park and are often taken home to trigger memories of park experiences, it is crucial for publications to convey as professional an appearance as possible. The overall look and feel of preserve produced publications will reflect consistency in design and style. A visual reference to the cultural presence at the preserve should also be included in the publication. Print quality, font and image selection and use, page layout, and other design basics will reflect the National Park Service standard (see www.graphics.nps.gov).

Develop a new unigrid brochure with Harpers Ferry Center. A new unigrid brochure is vital to the preserve's identity and to the visitor's experience. This new publication should give its readers a strong understanding of the preserve's national significance. It should create a visual link between the preserve and the National Park System. A sweeping front page photo will emphasize the big sky, the rolling landscape, and the diversity of the tallgrass prairie ecosystem. An introduction should summarize the preserve's purpose, highlight the history of its establishment, and explain its unique partnership. The preserve's interpretive themes—the natural history of prairie, the associated cultural history of Native Americans, and the legacy of ranching in the Flint Hills—should be cleverly presented. These intertwined stories can be clearly presented with text, captioned drawings, photographs, and illustrations. The reverse side should show a detailed preserve map, but can also feature inset maps or charts of interpretive value. All essential visitor information, safety messages, partner recognition, and contact information should be given as well.

Acquire publications training for at least one staff person. It is highly recommended that the Chief of Interpretation or other employee responsible for creating publications attend the training course, "Producing National Park Service Publications." This course covers basic information about the Messaging Project, publication design and theory, mapping, financial considerations, and other related material. It also provides opportunities to "talk shop" with instructors and other national park employees. Dynamic Graphics Educational Foundation (DGEF) in Peoria, Illinois (www.dgusa.com) includes some of the best training available for a range of media design and graphics education. Formal training can be supplemented with advice from other national park areas with similar stories and /or situations.

Acquire or develop additional products for sale in the preserve bookstore. The bookstore operator will be encouraged to continue offering the current products for sale and to seek appropriate new items to augment or replace existing inventory. Materials that interpret tallgrass prairie themes in a regional and global context would be appropriate. The current lack of site specific items suggests a focus on development of more of this type product. Development of the following appropriate non-traditional "publications" should be considered.

- Design, produce and sell a Tallgrass Prairie National Preserve patch in the preserve bookstore. The patch might include the visual image or logo proposed for outreach and arrival identity

- Design, produce and sell clothing (shirts, caps, windbreakers) that display thematic messages.

Develop a site-specific booklet on Tallgrass Prairie National Preserve. A small, moderately priced booklet will provide an affordable publication desired by most visitors. High color, profuse graphics and photographs, and minimal text will encourage use as visitors tour the preserve. This publication can also provide a high quality souvenir to share with friends and family and to assist in memorable experiences.

Develop a detailed handbook-type publication in partnership with other sites. Sales capacity and outlet at the preserve do not support the immense costs of producing a handbook featuring the preserve as the sole subject. However, the broad scope of stories related to preserve themes and resources go beyond preserve boundaries. A handbook that focuses on a particular theme and features complimentary stories from several parks could be a strong consideration for the future. For example, a handbook about cattle ranching could include stories about Tallgrass Prairie National Preserve, Grant-Kohrs Ranch National Historic Site, Theodore Roosevelt National Park, Homestead National Monument, and Lyndon B. Johnson National Historical Park. Detailed information and colorful photography can integrate landscapes and traditional cultures for people who want more information than provided in the preserve brochure.

Plan, develop and distribute a rack card publication. Travelers, commuters, vacationers, leisure drivers, and other passersby can easily be attracted to the preserve by effective rack cards placed at strategic locations such as rest areas, gas stations, motels, and chambers of commerce. Preserve staff can design this publication with a downloadable template from the National Park Service graphics identity website. The simplistic design carries the agency's strong identifiers of the black band and arrowhead. Coupled with a stunning photograph and effective text that offers information pertinent to travelers, these rack cards can be used as a marketing tool.

Plan, develop and distribute a series of site bulletins. Current site bulletins address the immediate needs of orienting visitors to sites and trails now open to the public. As preserve staff delves deeper into interpretive themes, site bulletins will play an important role in conveying information to the public. The following list describes some of the ten or more single sheet bulletins that will be needed to explore topics related to natural and cultural features at the preserve.

- Themes - A site bulletin can be developed for each of the preserve's five interpretive themes to explore the many subjects related to those themes. These bulletins can be distributed at visitor contact stations.

- Prairie Guide – Preserve staff should prepare a site bulletin that provides an introductory understanding of the prairie and identifies the most commonly seen plants and animals. The bulletin can be distributed at visitor contact stations and trailheads. The bulletin can include crisp photos or high-end illustrations, but should be designed to avoid competition with bookstore sales inventory.

- Understanding the Prairie - An overview of the deeper issues defining prairie, this bulletin could discuss the ice age, geology, extent of prairie, kinds of prairie, distinctive Flint Hills prairie characteristics, and prairie restoration and conservation techniques. Maps and diagrams will play an important part in telling this story. This can be offered at all visitor contact stations and trailheads.

- Development and Resource Management Projects - Temporary site bulletins might be developed to interpret on-going and changeable construction and natural or cultural resource activities that visitors might see. This bulletin can be distributed at visitor contact stations and project sites.

- Cultural Resources at the Preserve – An overview of the resources found at the preserve that signifies people on the land and how they shape their environment.

Research / Planning

Research and planning proposed for specific interpretive areas and specific media are described in sections of this plan that are dedicated to those areas and media. The following recommendations encompass a preserve-wide scope.

Interpretive manager will prepare implementation plans and goals annually. Each plan will present a comprehensive view of the annual interpretation and education program. Based on funding projections, these plans will briefly analyze the current program in relation to the long-range interpretive plan. The annual plan will identify management issues facing interpretation, propose an annual work plan, and describe new individual service plans. The plans will establish an annual program far enough in advance to allow efficient implementation.

Program and conduct natural, archeological, and historical research and adapt data for effective use by interpreters and visitors. Interpretation and education programming should be based on current research. Additional information about preserve resources and themes is needed to effectively plan and present activities. Such studies could include a comprehensive ethnobotony study, ethnographic oral and life histories, an ethnographic overview and assessment, and an ethnohistory of the preserve. Good information from nearby sites should be adapted for application at the preserve. Site specific information must be collected and adapted for presentation to visitors. Research knowledge should be made available to staff and other audiences in a useable format as soon as possible following acquisition.

Research and plan a variety of media to respond to visitor questions concerning natural history. Some visitor impressions of current natural resource themes are undoubtedly accurate. Many visitors might know that tall grass was unique in size and root structure. Some probably know that the tallest grasses would only occur in the bottomlands where the soil is deep and wet. Few realize that fire is an important natural resource management tool that has been used by all cultures that lived here. Media can interpret these and many other natural history stories hidden in the rolling Flint Hills. For example, if there is an on-going resource study, mention it in a preserve publication. The **APPENDICES** list typical visitor questions concerning natural resources that might need further exploration.

Research and develop a variety of media to respond to visitor questions concerning cultural diversity of people attracted to the tallgrass prairie region over the centuries from pre-history to today. American Indian, Euro-American (including Hispanic), African-American, Asian-American, and other peoples have used and benefited from the tallgrass prairie. Sometimes compelling stories of these people lie buried under traditional history of an area. African-American and Hispanic history at this preserve could have direct links to other national park sites in Kansas. Highlighting appropriate links to Brown v. Board of Education National Historic Site, Fort Scott National Historic Site, Fort Larned National Historic Site, and Nicodemus National Historic Site could help emphasize National Park Service identity state-wide. For example, finding answers to the questions about the Williams family (See **APPENDICES**) could result in interesting stories for presentation in state and national contexts.

Schedule and conduct studies to develop profiles of visitor interests and expectations. Because of changing demographics, scientific studies will be scheduled on a five to ten year cycle compatible with available budget. Frequent use of focus groups and other evaluation techniques described in **APPENDICES** will supplement cyclical studies to assure that interpretive services meet stakeholder need.

Wayside Exhibits

Develop a comprehensive wayside exhibit proposal and plan.
Preserve staff will work with Harpers Ferry Center to plan future wayside exhibit improvements based on the general management plan and Long-Range Interpretive Plan. Proposals will include exhibits and signs at the ranch headquarters, Lower Fox Creek School, Southwind Nature Trail, historic bottomland agricultural demonstration area, and appropriate locations in the upland prairie. Proposed exhibits will reflect Messaging Identity Project standards. The plan will propose exhibit locations, themes, objectives, topics, and site development. Some exhibits might incorporate audio and three dimensional elements.

Design, fabricate, and install permanent wayside exhibits and signs.
The preserve will work with Harpers Ferry Center to contract exhibit design and production. Design style and fabrication materials will reflect the five interpretive themes and the character of the preserve. Preserve staff will install exhibits at locations specified in the wayside exhibit plan and develop exhibit sites for convenient access by most visitors.

Create temporary wayside exhibits to interpret short term projects.
Construction, rehabilitation, resource management, and research projects in heavily used visitor areas can be identified and interpreted with wayside exhibits. Exhibits might explain about funding, partnerships, and future plans. For example "Facility improvements brought to you by a partnership between the National Park Service and the (insert private landowner's name). Currently work is being done to _____. Future projects include _____". Moveable exhibits can interpret temporary conditions. One movable exhibit might compare prescribed fires and wildfires to the traditional practice of range burning. These exhibits could be placed temporarily at appropriate locations within the preserve during and following either type of fire incident.

RANCH HEADQUARTERS COMPLEX

Visitor Experience Prescription – GMP

This interpretive area will serve as the primary focal point for the story of ranching in the Flint Hills region. Cultural resources will be the primary resource of concern.

The ranching character of the historic Spring Hill / Z Bar Ranch headquarters will be retained to the greatest extent possible. The ranch house, barn and associated outbuildings, and landscape features will be restored, rehabilitated, and/or preserved according to cultural landscape report and historic structures report recommendations. Historic grazing regimes and historic breeds of domesticated livestock will dominate the view seen from this area.

Interpretation and education activities associated with ranch operations in all seasons will help visitors understand the broad history of ranching in the Flint Hills. Activities may include staff-guided tours of historic buildings, self-guided activities such as walking nature trails, organized activities for school groups and bus tours, and demonstrations of historic farming and ranching practices. Wayside exhibits, publications, and interpretive and informational signs might also be used. A public transportation system on existing roads will provide transportation to various points, interpretive tours, and access to the prairie.

Recommendations

Arrival / Way-finding

Plan, produce and install a new entrance sign. A prominent and distinctive sign appropriate to the character of the preserve should leave no doubt as to the preserve's identity. The entrance sign should clearly state that this is Tallgrass Prairie National Preserve and a unit of the National Park Service. The visual image logo (National Park Service arrowhead) proposed in section **OUTREACH** should be repeated at the preserve entrance or at the information kiosk.

Utilize the information radio broadcast station located in Cottonwood Falls to broadcast specific interpretive program information, activities, and opportunities found at the preserve. Three stations located along the Flint Hills Scenic Byway will contact north and south bound travelers on Highway 177 as they enter the preserve and will welcome people to Tallgrass Prairie National Preserve on behalf of the National Park Service and the private landowner. Messages can introduce the partnership character of the preserve and describe visitor experience opportunities. An invitation to relax from highway travel will encourage people to stop to enjoy and learn about preserve resources. Information can easily be updated as appropriate to identify and encourage participation in special events.

Use the *Access Management Study and Plan* developed for the Kansas Department of Transportation to evaluate alternative solutions for identified safety problem of travelers stopping on highway in front of the ranch house. The study determined how best to accommodate or prevent stopping at this location. Alternatives evaluated would include a pull out or a sign that prohibits stopping. Signs from the north and south might state "No stopping on the highway". The current brown signs could be moved a greater distance from the entrance and present information identifying mileage to the entrance.

Allow a transitional experience without interpretive devices between the parking area and visitor contact station. Sensory experiences should dominate this area. Visitors will not have to be told that they are at a ranch – they can get that impression from the ambiance of historic structures, landscape, sounds, smells, and activity.

Improve and expand the self-guiding ranch headquarters walking tour brochure. This publication will enhance visitor exploration of the ranch headquarters landscape and structures. It can identify buildings and describe architectural features and functions. It might also describe hidden features, such as the ranch house historic water system, that add a sense of mystery. It can clarify unidentified features that prompt questions: what is that? Why did they do it that way? It could also include photographs of inaccessible areas.

Develop a uniform visual identity for signs and interpretive devices. The visual identity of directional signs and wayside exhibits should project a uniformity that reinforces the image first seen on arrival at the parking area. Visitors should be left with no doubt as to the preferred route from one interpretation site to another. Upon arrival at each interpretive feature (cultural or natural), the visitor should sense a uniformity in visual communication that relates to what he or she experienced when they first turned off the highway into this special place.

Plan, produce and install new interpretive wayside exhibits where appropriate, and remove existing waysides. A few wayside exhibits sensitively placed in the historic area can complement the self-guiding walking tour brochure. The following list identifies some of the potential exhibits that could be included in a revised wayside exhibit plan.

- Add a low profile trail head wayside exhibit behind the out house and within view of the Southwind Nature Trail head. The exhibit will welcome visitors to the prairie, present a map of the trail, and describe its length and difficulty.

- Produce and install a new wayside exhibit at the east side of the barn. The exhibit will interpret the barn and related structures and help guide the flow of foot traffic.

- Plan, produce and install a wayside that links the ecosystem of the prairie with the history of ranching on the prairie. Install this exhibit near the northwest corner of the barn where visitors can look west into the prairie.

Plan and produce an audio tour of the ranch headquarters complex. The audio can provide narration, historic dialogue, and sounds reflecting many stories related to ranching and farming in the tallgrass prairie. Audio on compact disk or other technology can be sold in the preserve bookstore for visitors to take home or rented with appropriate hardware for use while touring the ranch area.

Barn

Plan, produce, and install an orientation area on the second floor. Media will include information exhibits, personal service contact desk, and audiovisual kiosk. Until a visitor center is developed this section of the barn will provide the primary orientation to all preserve experience areas and introduction to all five interpretive themes during the summer. Orientation media and the contact desk will be moved to the ranch house when weather prohibits use of the barn. When preserve orientation is available at a visitor center this area will provide ranch orientation for visitors arriving by shuttle from that new facility.

Prepare an interim exhibit plan for the second floor. The plan can implement concepts identified in the long -range interpretive plan and created by preserve staff. It might include exhibits for the orientation area and for a museum exhibit area in another section of the barn. As a seasonal exhibition space the barn should never house any museum exhibits deemed essential to a visit to the preserve. Rotating and supplemental exhibits will account for the bulk of museum exhibits at this location.

Fabricate and install museum exhibits in a section of the second floor. Museum exhibits in the barn can effectively present topics related to the ranching legacy of the Flint Hills. The modular nature of proposed exhibit components that make them easy to produce or update by preserve staff should also contribute to their flexibility for various applications. Exhibits would be designed for compatibility with the rustic character of the barn. Exhibit components must also be rugged so they can survive the harsh atmosphere in this structure.

Because of this condition visitors should not be expected to endure lengthy interpretive messages. The following exhibit suggestions might prompt other ideas for museum exhibits in the barn.

- Tactile Boxes - Educational boxes on the floor or low tables for easy access by children will allow sensory exploration. Durable, safe items, such as a branding iron, prairie grasses, and horseshoe, can encourage children to see, feel, lift, and smell objects that facilitate physical and emotional connections to preserve stories.

- Ranching and Farming the Flint Hills – A permanent but mobile exhibit linking this ranch to all Flint Hills ranching activities could move to the Spring Hill Ranch house in the off -season when the barn is unavailable to visitors.

- Building Construction – Enhance the existing small exhibit with wood lathe by adding plaster to a portion of the lathe. Wallpaper on a small section of the plaster could show even more of the fabric in a typical wall.

- Stone Wall Building – A hands-on exhibit featuring simulation stone will invite visitors to try their skill at building a fence similar to those encountered on the preserve.

Develop a staging/gathering area on the second floor. This area would retain its historic barn character. Simple benches could accommodate school groups participating in curriculum-based education activities, people waiting for a bus tour of the prairie or walking tour of the ranch house, and groups arriving from the visitor center. The only permanent exhibits in this section of the barn would be tools and small equipment appropriate to reflect historic uses.

Plan and implement a living ranch program in the lower level of the barn. The lowest section along with outside corrals on the south and west side of the barn could provide a barn experience reflecting a working ranch. Here visitors could get close enough to see, hear, smell, and touch ranch animals. They might see and talk with a cowboy and perhaps even participate in simple ranching activities. Appropriate demonstrations and hands on activities could make the area an active experience. Whether visitors are self-guiding or participating in personal service activities, time spent in the living ranch area would provide a sense of being immersed in a real ranching operation. Few if any interpretive media other than personal services would be needed; make this an experience area.

Develop a visitor use plan for post visitor center operations. When development of a visitor center removes some functions from the barn, other uses must be considered. A visitor use planning project could propose appropriate uses. One idea for exploration might be expansion of living ranch activities from the lower level. Another could be extension of the museum exhibit area to provide more exhibits interpreting additional topics of Flint Hills ranching.

House

Adapt the barn orientation media for display in the ranch house during winter. The house orientation area will include information exhibits, display of the National Park Service arrowhead and preserve logo, personal service contact desk, and audiovisual kiosk. Until a visitor center is developed this section of the ranch house will provide the primary orientation to all preserve experience areas and introduction to all five interpretive themes during the winter.

Develop a variety of interpretive media for use in historic furnished spaces to supplement guided house tours. The primary method of showing the house will be guided narration, furnished spaces, and museum exhibits. Guided house tours will include a maximum of 12-15 visitors and the tour guide. Small interpretive panels can be kept in each room to help highlight different elements of the interpretation and to provide hands-on dimensions. These will be especially important for incompletely furnished areas. Preliminary ideas for supplemental media include historic wallpaper, faux finishes, moldings, music, and written or photographic evidence to show how rooms may be furnished.

Plan and produce an audiovisual program to provide visual access to inaccessible areas of the ranch house. The program could be presented in a kiosk in an accessible area of the house during winter and in the barn during summer. The program could run from a computer and present a ranger-led tour to provide mobility impaired visitors an opportunity to see the lower level of the house. This program could be run using DVD technology and utilize orientation video equipment, thus utilizing the same floor space.

Prepare a historic furnishings report for the Spring Hill Ranch house. Recommending a furnishings approach for the interior of the ranch house with real certainty is premature. To the extent historical evidence supports an 1881-1904 period of furnishings, it would be preferable to align with the period of national significance. Completion of a historic structures report, an assessment of the collections presently in the house, and a historic furnishings report should be taken into account in determining a period or periods of historic interiors.

Develop a visitor use plan for historic furnishings and traditional exhibits. The ranch house offers great options for mixed use of historic furnishings and traditional exhibits. The front door and a central stair hall accesses one group of rooms; the rear porch door best provides access to another set of rooms.

Prior to development of a visitor center and completion of the historic furnishings report, continue current use with more traditional exhibits supplementing displayed furnishings. See floor plans in **APPENDICES** for the following:

- Rooms 102 and 103: Add small interpretive exhibits sprinkled about to supplement current furnishings and personal services presented during house tours. Exhibits could present history (based on a timeline to help keep information clear for visitors) of the house, its residents, and their life on the ranch. These exhibits could be transferred to the second or third floor when a visitor center relieves the need for book/gift shop and office space here and the historic furnishings report provides evidence and documents recommendations as to how to fully furnish the ground floor of the home. Minimal exhibit units would work best in this space. Their portability would let them respond to experimentation to find the best traffic flow and would simplify the task of moving to a new space when the visitor center is constructed.

- Rooms 203 and 204: This area will continue operation as a preserve bookstore. This space needs to be a dedicated area that minimizes or eliminates sound and visual spill into other spaces.

- Room 202: This room will continue functioning as an audiovisual area during the winter. During the more temperate months when the audiovisual program is presented in the barn, the room can host a traditional exhibit or continue to house the Benninghoven period bedroom exhibit. The area might feature exhibits presenting topics of interest but not critical to have on display in all seasons. Subjects might include recent partnership projects between the preserve and nearby communities, quilts, school programs at the preserve, fence types, nonprofit landowner, and an oral history of the school. This area could be a testing space for exhibit ideas for the future visitor center. This is another space where the minimal exhibit modules would greatly contribute to effectiveness of interpretation. It might also be a space where a version of the simple modular exhibit case would be useful.

After development of a visitor center and completion of the historic furnishings report, increase historic furnishings and/or exhibits. Should the historic furnishings report unearth solid primary evidence for 1881-1904 interpretation, it will likely recommend that a sizeable portion of the house be historically furnished in this manner. Should the historic furnishings report find better primary evidence and/or original furnishings from a later 19th or early 20th century period, then the preserve might consider furnishing all or some portion of the house to that period.

- Room 102 and 103: In all likelihood, after the historic furnishings report, these rooms of the house will be furnished to the early period.

- Room 104, 105, 106, and 108: Interpretation of the rear first floor rooms should be determined after the historic structures report and the historic furnishings report are completed. These are fascinating spaces; interpretation should be compatible with accurate research data and treatment in other areas of the house.

- Room 202: Perhaps this room will be appropriate for furnishing to the early period to reflect Jones' ranch office.

- Rooms 204 and 203: These rooms would house exhibits interpreting the house, ranch life, and the residents. Visitors would enter from the rear of the house. The exhibit area could be separated from historically furnished areas by simply closing doors already in place. Should there be compelling historical evidence found for how the dining room (room 204) and the living room (room 203) were furnished in the late 19th/early 20th century these might be historically furnished and the exhibits would be located elsewhere. In the latter concept the exhibits could include more on the Benninghovens by featuring historical photographs of the third floor.

- Third Floor: If the historic furnishings report finds it appropriate, the third floor can be furnished to show the later period of the Benninghovens and/or earlier Jones period.

Outbuildings

Recommend replacement exhibits in a revised wayside exhibit plan. Remove all current wayside exhibits interpreting outbuildings

once new interpretive waysides are installed. A limited number of wayside exhibits might include the following:

- Produce and install a wayside interpreting the sod roof building.

- Produce and install a low profile wayside to the west of the outhouse. The exhibit might display a picture of the inside of the structure and emphasize the interesting interior features. The exhibit can interpret family life using the small toilet seat to reflect the parents' interest in their daughter.

Prepare a historic furnishings report for the ranch outbuildings. The report should be scheduled for completion after the historic structures report and historic furnishings plan for the main house are completed. These two reports will provide baseline research that need not be duplicated in a report for the outbuildings. Plan, produce and install appropriate furnishings or exhibits based on the outbuilding historic furnishings report.

Display items in the curing house in useful positions. Items for display should adhere to research findings in the historic furnishings report. Arrangement of objects should reflect historic uses to clearly reflect the function of the building.

LOWER FOX CREEK SCHOOL

Remove existing wayside exhibit; create a single new wayside. A new exhibit giving a very brief history of the school will reflect the most current research related to the school. It will match the identity standards established for all preserve wayside media. Install this exhibit closer to the beginning of the path connecting the parking area and the school building.

Install a viewing vestibule inside the school. Awareness of the ambience of this historic schoolroom will be greatly enhanced if visitors can physically stand within it. A vestibule at the front door would allow all visitors to see inside the school without assignment of preserve staff for security. Constructing a floor to ceiling barrier of Amiron glass (Schott Glass Company) or metal see-through fabric would enable this experience to take place, while preserving the fragile setting. A removable vestibule or a locked door in the vestibule wall can permit entry for interpreter-led groups. The step-in structure could be as large as five feet square if that size would not unduly impinge on the lay-out of the furnished school room. Additional lighting might be needed for the furnished area if glare makes looking through a glass vestibule difficult.

Prepare a historic furnishings report for the school. The report will ensure historic accuracy and document and justify furnishings. As this is to be a hands-on space for school groups, this project, and acquisition of objects for it, should be approached in a slightly different manner than most furnished areas. Based on the report and intended uses of the school building, the preserve staff might decide not to accession any of the furnishings as museum collections. The furnishings could be treated as education collections and include a high proportion of reproduction materials.

Furnish the interior of the school in accordance with historic furnishings report recommendations. Visitors to a furnished space could sense the atmosphere of a 19th century Flint Hills ranching community school. Historically accurate furnishings, building architecture, and surrounding landscape could trigger visitor visualization of education in a one-room schoolhouse on the Kansas prairie.

Research potential links to other sites and stories. Cross reference the Lower Fox Creek School with other schools, such as another Kansas school of great significance in a later era – Brown v. Board of Education National Historic Site. Did any African-American children ever attend the Lower Fox Creek School? Was there another area school attended by African-American children? Links to other areas could offer opportunities to interpret the school in a regional or national context.

Plan, produce and install a single, small interior exhibit to interpret the school. A moveable, free standing wayside exhibit or exhibit text and images mounted on a reader rail could interpret the furnished classroom. The exhibit would supplement furnishings so visitors would understand more about what they see. The exhibit could encourage cross-generational conversation and learning with minimal intrusion on the ambiance of the furnished interior.

A vandal resistant audio station concealed inside the school building could enhance visitor experience. This prescribed public space would lend itself to an ambient sound system creating historic classroom sounds or narration. The system could be actuated by a foot switch placed under a protective carpet in the vestibule. The system might include an on-demand microphone plug-in for use by preserve tour guides. An alternative video monitor could be considered in future planning. The preserve archives include a video tape of an interview with the last teacher at the school. An edited version might be shown in a small on-demand video kiosk.

Plan and present a variety of personal service activities at the school. Regularly scheduled and special activities could bring life to the school again. The school could be a spring board for a variety of education topics. Personal services could include on-demand education activities, special event living history or costumed interpretation, scheduled stationed assignment, and ranger-guided tours.

Continue and expand the Lower Fox Creek Schoolhouse Education Program. Education activities at the school will provide a core component of the preserve curriculum-based education program. Activities inside and outside the school building could include environmental education and historic school activities in a living classroom. Designated days during spring and fall could offer on-site opportunities to apply activities from a teacher's manual developed specifically for the school. Lesson plans and activities for teachers before and after their preserve visit could be available through the preserve web site.

Plan, produce and distribute a site bulletin featuring the school. The schoolhouse is a stand-alone site that can be discovered spontaneously by visitors. A site bulletin is needed to explain the structure and its significance. The publication would be appropriate for use in the school education program and for distribution to the public.

BOTTOMLAND PRAIRIE

Visitor Experience Prescription – GMP

Some fields within the Fox Creek riparian area will be restored to native vegetation. This will provide an example of a rare bottomland prairie community containing species common to deep, wet soil. This environment will allow for the survival of tallgrass species ranging in heights of six feet or more. Interpretation of this rare plant and animal community will focus on the pre-agricultural prairie ecosystem.

Agricultural crops may be reintroduced to some areas to reflect cultural landscapes and to supplement interpretation of ranching history.

Recommendations

Develop and present personal service interpretation and education activities for the three major elements of this area: riparian; prairie restoration; historic bottomland agricultural demonstration area. Appropriate activities include frequent informal roving, scheduled guided walks, occasional special events, hands-on education activities, and living history demonstrations.

Revise and update Bottomland Trail wayside exhibits as needed. The exhibits for this area are new and good quality. The following suggestions should be implemented during the next scheduled revision of wayside exhibits.

- Edit and relocate exhibits as needed to make them even more effective. Waysides are a site specific medium that captions the landscape; visitors should be able to look from the wayside to see or imagine directly in front of them the scene that the exhibit describes.

- Place more emphasis on natural history of bottomland prairie. Link prairie restoration, riparian environment, and plant and animal diversity to ranching as illustrated by cattle shipment and agricultural crop area.

- Develop a new wayside exhibit showing the depth and complexity of the tallgrass root structure and interpreting the significance of above and below ground relationships.

Plan and develop a new trail in the bottomland prairie. This foot trail could link the Bottomland Trail, historic bottomland agricultural demonstration area, visitor center, and ranch headquarters. A loop trail could include passage through the riparian area along Fox Creek and the bottomland prairie restoration area near Highway 177. Carefully placed standard cantilevered wayside exhibits at the headquarters and visitor center trail heads and small trailside exhibits along the trail will enhance visitor experience.

Include specific recommendations for interpretation of the historic bottomland agricultural demonstration area in plans developed for that area. The sampling of historic orchards, gardens, and crops can be interpreted by small trailside wayside exhibits, a walking tour site bulletin, and scheduled guided tours or cultural demonstrations.

Develop a wildflower program in partnership with regional youth organizations. Local school children or 4-H groups might volunteer to develop and coordinate a wildflower program for the bottomland prairie. A limestone circular planter in the developed area at the parking lot could provide an activity site introducing flowering plants that might be discovered growing wild in the prairie, as well as teach children about the cultural aspects of plants. Other activities throughout the bottomland prairie interpretive area could teach children about wildflowers, grasses, and the animals that depend on them.

UPLAND PRAIRIE

Visitor Experience Prescription – GMP

The emphasis in this area will be management of the prairie through use of fire, cattle, and bison, while providing a variety of visitor experience opportunities. Prairie management will create a landscape mosaic to help maintain and enhance the variety of native plant and animal life associated with the tallgrass prairie. Historic and contemporary grazing regimes will allow interpretation of the continuum of ranching in the Flint Hills. Visitors will be able to see cattle and bison and learn about their effects on the prairie.

Non-motorized visitor access to the prairie will be by existing ranch roads. Limited backcountry hiking and primitive camping may be allowed to offer a high quality experience. Interpretation and education efforts will consist primarily of staff conducted interpretive bus tours and publications. Other interpretation and education activities will be minimal.

Recommendations

Interpretation on Southwind Nature Trail connects the ranch headquarters complex to upland prairie. The loop trail provides good views of the schoolhouse, rock fences, creek valley, and rolling hills. Interpretation can emphasize those views to link the fenced ranching era illustrated by the ranch headquarters to pre-ranching upland prairie environments. The focus of the trail should be to create a transition between the headquarters and upland interpretive areas.

Plan and produce a trail guide publication for Southwind Nature Trail. The guide will provide trail information and interpretation arranged in a reverse time line that integrates people and prairie. Interpretive content should start with a brief statement about ranching stories that visitors have already experienced in the headquarters area. Interpretation could transition to an introduction of pre-ranching prairie. People of the Prairie could convey the relationship between American Indians and the prairie. There must be rich quotes, storytelling, and other oral history that can put a colorful spin on the land of tall grasses. The trail guide should conclude with an introduction to the pre-human prairie ecosystem to direct visitor interest toward exploring the backcountry hiking area of the prairie beyond the Southwind Nature Trail.

Remove Southwind Nature Trail wayside exhibits at the overlook area; plan, produce and install a new low profile trailhead wayside behind the historic outhouse. Place a new trail sign exhibit closer to the beginning of the trail. Consider leaving the overlook area as a quiet open spot for relaxation and reflection without exhibits. The trail guide publication described previously can provide interpretation. If a wayside exhibit must be located at the overlook, it should depict the view from this vantage point before settlement by Euro-Americans. The exhibit could present a painting that populates the scene with American Indians and buffalo.

Plan, produce and distribute a site bulletin for the upland prairie/ranching interpretive area. The publication would encourage and facilitate self-guided exploration of the tallgrass landscape on designated paths. It would help visitors understand a historic Kansas cattle ranch that is dependent upon weather, water, and fire. The site bulletin could include a map of ranch roads useful as walking trails. It could interpret the raising of cattle, bison grazing, and small plots that may be established for resource management or education activities. A few small trailside site identification exhibits might supplement the bulletin if they can be positioned unobtrusively, perhaps at ranch road gates.

Schedule guided bus tours of the prairie to reflect visitation patterns. Visitors who travel through the preserve on a bus tour have many opportunities for immersion in the prairie landscape. Views provide a physical, visual link to landscapes experienced by native peoples, settlers, early ranch owners and workers. Narration by tour guides help visitors understand stories that are not easily seen in the current landscape. Topics might include pre-ranching prairie environment and an expansion of American Indian stories introduced to visitors on the Southwind Nature Trail. Bus pick-up and drop-off might be located at the west end of the barn to avoid modern vehicle travel through the headquarters. Staff will find consistent ways to reduce or limit visitor impact to prehistoric resources in the preserve.

Plan and present a limited special event personal service program.

- Schedule occasional hikes or special bus tours. One event could feature a visit to several management plots and interpretation of alternative management practices that demonstrate the effects of various actions on the tallgrass prairie.

- Provide wagon rides or horseback rides into the upland prairie to interpret historic activities that occurred at the ranch. Preserve staff could contact other sites that currently have or have had such programs for ideas: Lyndon B. Johnson National Historical Park, Iowa Living History Farms, and Old World Wisconsin. The Association of Living Historical Farms and Agricultural Museums provides training for interpretation, historic research and accuracy, and living history farms.

DAY USE AREA

Visitor Experience Prescription – GMP

This area will include the lands east of the Fox Creek bottomland prairie and the agricultural areas adjacent to the east/west county road. Resources, facilities and a variety of activities will offer day use opportunities for visitors to explore the preserve and learn about the tallgrass prairie, its associated ranching history, and American Indian cultures. A range of non-motorized day use activities such as hiking, horseback riding, or fishing will be permitted if impacts to natural and cultural resources can be managed and conflicts among users minimized.

Recommendations

Plan, produce, and install orientation exhibits at major access point. A wayside exhibit kiosk will shelter upright wayside exhibits and provide shade for people. One exhibit will provide detailed orientation, basic interpretation and directions to nearby points of interest. A second panel can interpret resource features near the kiosk in relation to a preserve-wide and ecosystem context. The exhibit kiosk will also present safety and regulation information, Leave No Trace minimum impact techniques, and resource management issues specific to the day use interpretive area.

Plan, produce, and install trail head exhibits at hiking and horse-back riding trails. Planning for any future trails that may be developed in the day use area should include specific recommendations for trail head exhibits. Site-specific exhibits at each trail head will identify trail route, length, difficulty, estimated time, and safety considerations and present photographs of features that can be seen from the trail.

Plan, produce, and install interpretive wayside exhibits. Interpretive exhibits should be placed in heavily used areas. Low profile exhibit panels will provide interpretation near parking areas and on short walking trails that might be developed in the future. Longer trails will feature small, lesser intrusive trailside exhibits to identify specific resources and topics.

Develop and present personal service interpretation and education activities. Appropriate activities include frequent informal roving, occasional special events and scheduled hikes, and education activities when requested.

West view of the prairie from inside the historic limestone barn.

VISITOR CENTER

Visitor Experience Prescription – GMP

A multi-purpose visitor center will complement visitor services located in other areas of the preserve and nearby communities. The visitor center will provide the initial stop for visitors, allowing them easy access to basic information about the preserve and community resources and services, and enabling them to orient themselves and plan their visit. It will also be a primary staging area for the public transportation system and for basic education and interpretation that will focus on orientation, information, preserve interpretive themes, and bookstore sales.

Visitor movement and access in this interpretive area will be controlled to ensure resource protection, while accommodating high density use. These controls may include improvements such as walkways, barriers, benches, and interpretive and informational signs.

Recommendations

A new visitor center should be constructed to provide initial orientation to the preserve and interpretation of preserve themes. It will present the preserve as a scenic cultural landscape shaped by natural processes and human forces to provide habitat for a diversity of plants and animals. It will provide concise, basic information that lets visitors move into the preserve quickly to meet their needs. It will also offer opportunity to obtain detailed information and interpretation for visitors who have more time to spend in the visitor center.

Exterior Spaces

The visitor center will be sited to offer greater visitor access to all facilities and within easy range to the historic corridor. The preferred site would be a primary highway. Highway signs could tell travelers about the visitor center, identify its name, and show the distance from that sign's location to the facility. The building should be clearly identified as a National Park Service facility. Design of the structure must present an attractive appearance, yet not intrude upon the prairie or historic scene from other key sites in the preserve. One such element could be a sod roof and limestone face that mimics the historic chicken house. The design of roads, parking areas, and sidewalks should make navigation to the center building intuitive and easy for visitors to follow.

The visitor center will be sited to provide the best view of preserve resources as possible and greater access to visitor opportunities. A preferred site criterion is to offer a view into the preserve without impeding on the historic buildings. Adjacent parcels of land with high potential for development would leave the visitor center site in a vulnerable position. In such case, care should be taken to ensure that design of the visitor center does not require that the adjacent land stay in its present state. For example, visitor center windows or viewing decks should not be designed to face onto privately owned land that may be developed after visitor center construction.

Parking areas will be adequate to accommodate staff and public automobiles, recreational vehicles and commercial buses. Parking and circulation space will include a staging area for the preserve shuttle vehicles.

Outdoor information exhibits between the parking area and the visitor center entrance will provide basic self-service orientation for visitors who arrive when the building is closed or who choose not to go inside the center.

The architecture of the building will reflect the natural and cultural environment of the preserve's resources, while incorporating sustainable practices. The facility will reflect in design, finishes, colors, and media treatments the major themes reflected in preserve resources. Structural design will facilitate visitor movement through the developed area.

A landscaped plaza adjacent to the visitor center can create a transitional experience between developed and natural/historical environments. Experience pods in the landscaped plaza will provide "outdoor rooms" with decks, walks or short trails, seating zones and casual use areas. Pods will be suitable for assembling groups of varying sizes for interpretive activities and special events, for staging areas, linkage between visitor center and backcountry day hiking trails, historic building corridor, amphitheater, or for spaces simply to relax. Landscaping could create opportunities for visitors to choose to be in the sun or in the shade.

Interior Spaces

An introductory space near the visitor center entrance will welcome visitors to this partnership national park area. An exhibit will identify Tallgrass Prairie National Preserve, the primary landowner, and the National Park Service. Media, architecture, signs and possibly sculptural elements will introduce the missions of the managing organizations and state the significance of their partnership.

Visitors will first enter a lobby for information and directions to other parts of the building and preserve. Information related to travel, accessibility, visiting options, and preserve features will be offered in a variety of media formats, including an information desk with personal services. Orientation exhibits will identify where visitors are located in relation to other preserve sites. Information exhibits will describe preserve-wide experience opportunities from which visitors can choose to meet their individual needs. Sufficient circulation space will be provided for users to move among functional areas without congestion. Comfortable seating will be available for mobility impaired visitors and those wanting a casual experience.

A museum exhibit space should be adjacent to the lobby, but designed to prevent sound spill from that noisy space. There should be no windows in the exhibit room so fluctuations of light produced by the sun can be eliminated. The space should have at least a ten foot high ceiling and a floor size to accommodate exhibits interpreting all five preserve themes. Exhibit concepts to integrate media and themes in this space are described in section **"Museum Exhibit Recommendations."**

A theater will be dedicated to audiovisual and formal presentations. A sloped floor and formal, comfortable seating would improve viewing quality. Space for a small stage, either fixed or moveable, should be provided at the front of the theater. A projection system should accept current technology software and storage media including public address and video, motion picture, and computer generated projection. Storage space would accommodate backup equipment and supplies. Controls should allow operation of audiovisual equipment from the information desk, projection booth if supplied, and from the front of the theater. The theater would be the primary location for showing the film described in **"PRESERVE-WIDE RECOMMENDATIONS - Audiovisual"** section of this plan.

A sales area to support and extend interpretive opportunities should be located out of the main circulation path but easily seen from the lobby. A cash register at a sales desk, a storage area for inventory, security safe and work space should be located convenient to the sales area. Space dedicated to display and circulation would be large enough to encourage people to browse.

A multipurpose room should be furnished with moveable seating, work tables and audiovisual capabilities. This space could accommodate temporary exhibits, education activities, meetings, training, and interpretive programs that cannot be presented outside.

Facility designers must plan public and staff restroom size and location to adequately serve the anticipated users. Features near public rest rooms should include water fountains and public telephones. Staff restrooms should include space for changing and storing clothing during cultural demonstrations and other functions.

Offices should accommodate the number of staff required to operate the visitor center. Support space would be available for mailroom, copier, fax, office supplies, computer, scanner, printer, break room, and interpretive program preparation.

A museum storage area would house all museum objects in the preserve collection. The storage facility must be sited above the 500-year flood plain.

Library space of sufficient size to accommodate current and projected library collection (book, journal, photo/slide) should also include a computer work station.

Maintenance and storage would occupy two rooms or locking areas. A janitorial wet section should be separated from a dry maintenance storage area.

Museum Exhibit Recommendations

Exhibits in the visitor center should introduce all interpretive themes but focus on themes other than ranching. This approach would tend to balance thematic interpretation throughout the preserve. The ranching theme will be extensively interpreted at the ranch headquarters complex. The visitor center will extensively interpret the prairie and its natural and cultural history.

Exhibit units would have a clear organizational principle, but should not require visitors to follow a set sequence.

Develop a museum exhibit proposal, design and production plan for the center. The plan would detail exhibit descriptions, exhibit room layout and selection of media, artifacts, objects, and content.

Exhibit planners will consider the following ideas for exhibits when completing the visitor center exhibit plan.

- Tallgrass Prairie: What is tallgrass? Where and why does it grow? How has the prairie changed? What factors affect the prairie in the Flint Hills of Kansas?

- How Tall Is Tall?: Correct the misconception that tallgrass must be seven feet high everywhere.

- Continuum of human history: Reflect the different time periods and phases of development of tallgrass prairies using preserve resources as examples.

- American Indian: Explore what is known (archeology from 12000 years ago to present; quarry sites on upland; small villages on bottomland 3000 years ago) and the mysteries still to be solved as archeology research continues.

- Geology: Text, graphics, and camera or computer generated animation could show how geology made the tallgrass prairie landscape possible.

- Cattle ranching: How has ranching effected the natural environment of the Flint Hills tallgrass prairie over time? How have the different eras and types of ranching affected the local, regional and national way of life and the local, regional, and national economy? What influence has the railroad had on the Flint Hills area? How did the Flint Hills become connected with other communities in the region and nation through railroad use?

- Computer generated topographical map: A multi-dimensional map on a square pedestal base with audiovisual capabilities can show the cultural and natural areas of the preserve. The exhibit should be placed in the visitor center museum. A wide range of topics could be displayed using different colored lights under the raised Plexiglas topographical map. Topics displayed could range from land ownership and acquisition, upland prairie, bottomland prairie, riparian areas, outline of the preserve, evolution of the preserve landscape, hiking, backcountry and other activities.

- Role of fire: Design an interactive video simulation game like Sim City or Ontario Science Center's forest fire game. Name it Sim Prairie or Sim Rancher. In addition to display as a museum exhibit, the product could be sold in the bookstore. Simulation could interpret the variables critical to current and historic types of prairie management – fire, cattle and bison grazing, open and closed range, different grazing regimes, wind, weather, and geology.

- Spring Hill Ranch: A minor exhibit element strategically placed at the visitor center should pique interest of visitors on their way to the historic ranch headquarters and also provide information for those without the time to go to the ranch.

- Changing Exhibits: These exhibits could interpret special issues, seasonal experience opportunities, or reflect evolving research and management activities. Changing exhibits especially benefit local, repeat visitors.

- Museum Dioramas: Show the tallgrass prairie root system and tallgrass, "historic plow vs. the Flint Hills", and other themes as appropriate.

- Prairie Murals: Large-format photographs placed on the museum walls could show the expansive views of the prairie to help visitors become engrossed with the tallgrass prairie ecosystem.

Produce and install museum exhibits described in the museum exhibit plan. Integrated themes would provide a context for learning experiences throughout the preserve. The exhibits would also integrate media to provide a good balance of interactive tactile and graphic elements interspersed with short audio and video.

IMPLEMENTATION PLAN

The implementation plan summarizes proposals presented in this long-range interpretive plan, establishes priorities, identifies possible funding sources, describes some design and production considerations and recommends evaluation methods. The preserve staff will develop necessary funding requests to begin the federal funding process. They will also initiate contacts with potential partnership organizations to implement projects well suited to alternative funding.

Estimated Class C Costs in 2005 dollars

PROJECT SCHEDULE / SUMMARY

Outreach

Project	PMIS #	Details	Total Cost	FY 2006	FY 2007	FY 2008	FY 2009	FY 2010 & beyond
Expand Website Capabilities (pages 41-42)		Add Quick Time VR 360 degree views of the prairie, audio and video clips, provide virtual tours of the buildings and the prairie, on-line Jr. Ranger program, and educational activities for teachers and children.	$20,000	Program ongoing, expansion contingent on funding				
Expand Community Outreach Program (pages 42 and 48)		Develop, coordinate, and present personal services and activities to nearby communities and special populations on various topics of the preserve.		Skeleton program implemented; expansion based on funding				
Traveling Trunks (pages 42-43)		Continue development and marketing of the traveling trunk program using curriculum-based activities. Ten traveling trunks will be developed surrounding the parks five interpretive themes. Two trunks per year will be developed. Included in the trunks will be a resource handbook, props, videos, CDs, books, and other appropriate materials.	$25,000 total	▭	▭	▭	▭	▭
Traveling Exhibits (page 42)		Plan and develop traveling exhibits such as a Prairie Discovery Center for appropriate audiences and sites. Exhibits would be used to attend trade shows and off-site programs.	$10,000			▭		

Tallgrass Prairie National Preserve Long-Range Interpretive Plan

Outreach continued

Project	PMIS #	Details	Total Cost	FY 2006	FY 2007	FY 2008	FY 2009	FY 2010 & beyond
Partnership Opportunities (pages 53-54)		Partner with local communities, government agencies, nonprofit organizations, primary landowning partner, and others to assist in reaching the desired future conditions of the preserve by pursuing grants in support of interpretive and educational activities and sales items. Partner with other prairie and ranching National Park units to share in activities and funding for marketing, training, research, special events and seminars, and other opportunities.	Costs incorporated into base funds					
American Indian Partnerships (page 54)		Explore potential to establish and maintain strong partnerships to effectively tell stories related to the preserve of early inhabitants and tribal culture.	$10,000 travel costs	Program On-going				
Volunteer Opportunities (page 54)	109105	Enlist school groups, scouts, volunteer groups, individuals, and others to assist with resource restoration activities and special events. Work with 4-H groups and other groups in volunteer activities supporting education programs.	$6,000 travel costs	Program On-going				
Partner with Educational Institutions and Organizations (page 54)		Partner with educational institutions and organizations to assist with historic research, professional assessment of natural and cultural resources, and other projects as required.	Costs covered by project funds	Program On-going				

Tallgrass Prairie National Preserve Long-Range Interpretive Plan

Exhibits

Project	PMIS #	Details	Total Cost	FY 2006	FY 2007	FY 2008	FY 2009	FY 2010 & beyond
Develop Museum Exhibits for Barn and Ranch House (pages 46, 47, 65, and 66)		Preserve staff will plan and produce orientation and interpretive exhibits to serve visitors at the historic ranch headquarters until a visitor center is developed. After a visitor center is developed, exhibits will be concentrated in new facility.	$15,000 pre-visitor center $500,000 post-visitor center	Pre-visitor center	Pre-visitor center	Pre-visitor center	Post-visitor center	Post-visitor center
Curing House Exhibits (page 70)		Display items in useful positions based on research findings from the Historic Furnishings Report.			▓	▓	▓	
New Orientation Area in Barn (page 65)		Plan, produce, and install new orientation area on second floor of barn. Media will include new exhibits, contact station desk, and audiovisual kiosk. Kiosk project is listed in Media Section.	$10,000		▓	▓	▓	
Preserve Exhibit Program Plans (pages 46 – 47)		Develop pre-visitor center exhibit and activity program plans for orientation, information, and interpretive exhibits for all visitor use areas.	Cost will be incorporated into base funding.		▓	▓		
Post Visitor Center Plan (pages 46 and 67)		Develop a visitor use plan for post visitor center operations. Explore the possibility of extending the living ranch activities located in the first floor of the barn to the second floor.	Cost will be incorporated into base funding.				▓	

Tallgrass Prairie National Preserve Long-Range Interpretive Plan

Exhibits continued

Project	PMIS #	Details	Total Cost	FY 2006	FY 2007	FY 2008	FY 2009	FY 2010 & beyond
Barn Exhibit Plan (page 65)		Prepare an interim exhibit plan for the second floor of the barn including orientation area and museum exhibit area. Staff will develop.	Cost will be incorporated into base funding.		██	██	██	██
Museum Exhibits on Second Floor of Barn (pages 65-66)		Goal is to present topics related to the ranching legacy through hands-on activities such as tactile boxes, mobile exhibits, rock wall construction activities, and more.	$10,000		██	██	██	
Develop Staging Area in Barn (page 66)		Using historically appropriate benches, develop a staging area for people waiting for tours or educational activities.	$3,000			██	██	
Historic Furnishings / Exhibits (pages 68-69)		Increase historic furnishings and/or exhibits based on solid primary evidence for the period of significance.	Cost contingent on findings of the Historic Furnishings Report					
Vestibule in School (pages 71-72)		Install a viewing vestibule inside Lower Fox Creek School.	$10,000	██	██			
School Furnishings (page 72)		Furnish the interior of the school according to the Historic Furnishings Report recommendations.	Cost contingent on findings of the Historic Furnishings Report					

Exhibits continued

Project	PMIS #	Details	Total Cost	FY 2006	FY 2007	FY 2008	FY 2009	FY 2010 & beyond
Interior Exhibit in School (pages 72-73)		Plan, produce, and install a small interior exhibit to interpret the school.	$2,000					
Interpretive Media/Exhibit in House (page 67)		Develop interpretive media and traditional exhibits for use in historically furnished spaces to supplement guided house tours and current furnishings.	$4000					

Formal Interpretation and Education

Project	PMIS #	Details	Total Cost	FY 2006	FY 2007	FY 2008	FY 2009	FY 2010 & beyond
Expand School Education Program (pages 51 and 73)		Expand Lower Fox Creek curriculum-based education program with more supplies, period costumes, and teacher handbooks. Offer special spring and fall days for on-site activities from a teacher's manual developed for the school.	$10,000 supplies, printing, & costumes	Upgrade	Program continues to develop			
Develop More Natural and Cultural Activities (pages 45-46)		Interpretive activities will include more programs based around the natural and cultural dynamics of the tallgrass prairie ecosystem. Such programs targeted around prairie grass root systems, insects, mammals, American Indian culture, ranching, and more.	$20,000 for supplies	On-going activities – Special Interpretive Programs				
Image Reference File (page 49)		Create and continually augment reference file of images pertaining to the preserve, including historic photos.	$5,000 for supplies/ training.					
Curriculum-Based Educational Activities (pages 50-51)		Education programs will fit established Kansas curricula and reflect national standards in immersion activities. Handouts will be available on-line for pre and post-visit activities to reinforce learning experiences. New activities will reflect real-life applications and will be compatible with current school requirements and learning styles.	$30,000 for supplies and training	Program continues to develop and standards are met upon completion of				

Tallgrass Prairie National Preserve Long-Range Interpretive Plan

Formal Interpretation and Education continued

Project	PMIS #	Details	Total Cost	FY 2006	FY 2007	FY 2008	FY 2009	FY 2010 & beyond
Explore Distance Learning Activities (page 51)		Staff will explore possibilities of distance learning with regional schools and national educational organizations using the internet as a medium.	$25,000			■	■	■
Education Specialist (page 52)		Education Specialist will coordinate curriculum-based education program and attend workshops and meetings to bring more educational opportunities to the preserve.	Park base increase required for new position.			■	■	■
Establish Education Group (page 52)		Preserve staff will establish an education advisory group (teachers) to assist with development of programs and new educational activities, assuring that the programs align with classroom requirements and state's current schedule of assessments.	$10,000		■	■	■	■
Implement Training and Internship Program with Teachers and Educational Partners (pages 52)		Goal is to train teachers and student teachers about the preserve so they can independently present educational activities based on preserve themes. Explore opportunities to establish a cooperative program with local colleges and universities to offer student teacher internships and training.	$20,000			■	■	

Formal Interpretation and Education continued

Project	PMIS #	Details	Total Cost	FY 2006	FY 2007	FY 2008	FY 2009	FY 2010 & beyond
Continue to Improve Current Personal Service Activities and Develop New Activities (pages 54, 55, and 81)		Goal is to maintain and improve the current personal services such as house and bus tours, education programs, and stationed assignments. Routinely evaluate all personal service activities and adapt as needed to assure thematic depth and diversity. Other activities will include frequent informal roving, scheduled hikes, and special activities.	$90,000 for six additional seasonal staff					
Plan and Present Series of Special Events (page 55)		Preserve will sponsor or assist with special events both on and off-site. Each event will be based around preserve themes. Such events as cultural music programs, holiday events, harvest festivals, prairie days, and night sky programs.	$50,000					
Children's Program Series (page 55)		Goal is to develop special days for children to visit the preserve and experience the resources with activities geared toward the appropriate age level.	$5,000					
Develop Living History Program (page 55)		Develop elements of the living history program that would be presented in first person format. Programs would be presented in the ranch headquarters and schoolhouse areas.	$75,000 for costumes and equipment					

Formal Interpretation and Education continued

Project	PMIS #	Details	Total Cost	FY 2006	FY 2007	FY 2008	FY 2009	FY 2010 & beyond
Develop Staff Training Program (pages 55–56)		Training program will include components that focus on content, accuracy, completeness, and interpretive and communication skills necessary for presenting programs and activities. Bring in National Park Service trainers versed in the Interpretive Development Program.	$10,000		▉	▉		
Living Ranch Program in Barn (pages 66–67)		Enhance the visitor experience by having animals in the lowest level of the barn, corral area, and pastures south of the barn. Visitor can hear, see, smell, and possibly touch animals as part of their ranching experience, while visiting with an interpreter.	$100,000 for livestock, supplies & 1 FTE					▉
Present Special Activities at the School (page 73)		The historic school will be a spring board for a variety of educational topics. Such activities could include special events, living history costumed activities and interpretation, and ranger guided tours.	$10,000			▉	▉	▉
Develop Funding Strategies (page 53)		Seek funds for implementing additional educational programs for current and future demands. Create an interdisciplinary team of staff to identify cross-division projects and funding sources.	$8,000 travel		▉	▉	▉	

Tallgrass Prairie National Preserve Long-Range Interpretive Plan

Formal Interpretation and Education continued

Project	PMIS #	Details	Total Cost	FY 2006	FY 2007	FY 2008	FY 2009	FY 2010 & beyond
Research Education Links (page 72)		Cross reference the Lower Fox Creek school with other schools to explore the possibilities of interpreting the school at a regional or national level. Develop partnerships for educational activities and opportunities.	$3,000					
Bus and Wagon Tours of the Prairie (page 79)		Continue scheduled guided bus tours to reflect visitor patterns and augment with wagon rides on special occasions as visitors gain a deeper understanding of the openness of the prairie.

Add two new buses to the interpretive fleet. | $300,000 | | | | | |

Publications

Project	PMIS #	Details	Total Cost	FY 2006	FY 2007	FY 2008	FY 2009	FY 2010 & beyond
Expand Hiking Trail Maps (page 78)		Develop new hiking trail maps for the Southwind Nature Trail and Bottomland Trail using the Messaging Project guidelines.	$16,000	▓	▓	▓		
Site Bulletins (pages 58-59, and 78)		Develop and print site bulletin series on subjects relating to preserve themes. Areas would include the schoolhouse, trails, ranching legacy, tallgrass prairie ecosystem, cultural resources, and more. Site bulletins will be developed using the Messaging Project guidelines and in several languages.	$40,000 printing costs	Program on-going and more site bulletins will be produced as research uncovers further information.				
Develop Park Unigrid Brochure (pages 56-57)		Develop a unigrid brochure for the preserve through Harpers Ferry Center (HFC). The preserve has been accepted into the Unigrid Brochure program, with completion scheduled by spring 2007. Currently the preserve distributes a color brochure that was developed in partnership with the preserve's partner.	HFC Funded Initially $8,000 printing costs		▓			
Publications Training (page 57)		Send one staff member to the training course "Producing National Park Service Publications."	$1,000	▓				
Site Specific Books (page 58)		Develop a site-specific booklet on the preserve and a detailed handbook publication in partnership with other sites.	$72,000			▓	▓	▓

Publications continued

Project	PMIS #	Details	Total Cost	FY 2006	FY 2007	FY 2008	FY 2009	FY 2010 & beyond
Self-Guiding Brochure (page 64)		Expand and print the current self-guiding historic ranch headquarters walking tour brochure. Brochure will enhance visitor exploration of the ranch landscape and structures.	$8,000 Cost On-going					
Backcountry Hiking Guide (page 78)		Develop and print hiking map and brochure to guide visitors safely into the backcountry areas of the preserve.	$8,000 Cost On-going					

Media

Project	PMIS #	Details	Total Cost	FY 2006	FY 2007	FY 2008	FY 2009	FY 2010 & beyond
Accessibility Kiosk (pages 48, 67, and 68)	92315	Design, fabricate, and install an interactive video kiosk to allow access to less accessible areas of the house, barn, and prairie. Quick Time Virtual Reality clips of these areas will be used.	$27,000		�In			
Barn Orientation Media (page 67)		Adapt barn orientation media for display in the ranch house during winter. Assurance should be made that this requirement is incorporated into other projects during the planning stages.	$5,000		▐			
Audio Station in School (page 73)		Install a vandal resistant audio station inside the school to enhance visitor experience. A foot switch placed under protective carpet in the vestibule or motion activated device could activate sounds and narration of a normal one-room school.	$5,000				▐	
Audio Tour of Ranch Headquarters (page 65)		Plan and produce an audio tour via headset that can be rented from the visitor contact station. Visitors will hear historic dialogue, ranch sounds, etc. Audio tour will be available in English and Spanish.	$60,000 for production, headsets, research, and taping.			▐		▐

103

Tallgrass Prairie National Preserve Long-Range Interpretive Plan

Waysides and Signs

Project	PMIS #	Details	Total Cost	FY 2006	FY 2007	FY 2008	FY 2009	FY 2010 & beyond
Highway Signs (pages 42 and 84)		Develop preserve highway signage plan to improve way finding. Plan has been developed and is awaiting implementation through the Kansas Dept. of Transportation (KDOT) and Kansas Tourism Department. Signs will display the National Park Service arrowhead.	No cost to the preserve. Working with KDOT for signage.	Complete by end of this fiscal year.				
Scenic Route to the Preserve (page 42)		Use existing Kansas Highway 177 (Scenic Byway) to develop a connection between the preserve and the Santa Fe Trail at Council Grove.	$5,000 signage				▯	
Wayside Exhibit Plan and Exhibits (pages 61, 64, 70, and 71)	92314	Develop a comprehensive wayside exhibit proposal and plan with Harpers Ferry Center. Work with HFC to design and fabricate wayside exhibits and signs. Signs and interpretive devices will clearly identify a visual uniformity. Currently used waysides will be removed when new waysides are installed. Waysides are for the headquarters area, prairie overlook area, Southwind Nature Trail, bottomland cultural area, and schoolhouse area.	$135,000		▯			
Temporary Wayside Exhibits (page 61)		Create temporary wayside exhibits for short-term projects. Banners with removable vinyl may be used on a temporary basis.	$5000		▯			
New Entrance Sign – See Visitor Center								

Waysides and Signs continued

Project	PMIS #	Details	Total Cost	FY 2006	FY 2007	FY 2008	FY 2009	FY 2010 & beyond
Expand/Supplement Bottomland Trail Waysides (page 75)		The wayside exhibits were installed in FY 2004. Expand and supplement these exhibits as needed. Develop new exhibit showing the depth and complexity of the root system as part of the exhibits at the preserve.	$12,000					
Exhibit Kiosk in Day Use Area (pages 80-81)		Plan, produce, and install orientation exhibits at major access points, trailheads, or other areas where safety messages would be beneficial. Trail descriptions on trailhead exhibits will include levels of access, safety and regulation information, Leave No Trace techniques, and resource management issues.	$15,000					

Research and Planning Documents

Project	PMIS #	Details	Total Cost	FY 2006	FY 2007	FY 2008	FY 2009	FY 2010 & beyond
Historic Furnishings Report for the Ranch House, Barn, Schoolhouse, and Outbuildings (pages 47, 68-70, and 72)		Historic Furnishings Report for visitor use areas that will feature accurately furnished spaces. Current furnishings will be evaluated and additional furnishings will be recommended to enhance historic appearances. Plan will determine a period of interpretation and aid in acquisition of items for the permanent collection.	$75,000 for all reports		▮			
Visitor Use Plan (page 47)		Based on the Historic Furnishings Report a visitor use plan will be developed for historic furnishings and traditional exhibits. The ranch house offers great options for mixed use of historic furnishings and traditional exhibits. The plan will include design elements, graphics, and label/copy as appropriate.	$10,000				▮	
Scope of Collections Statement (page 50)		Complete Scope of Collections Statement.			▮			
Implementation Plans and Goals Annually (page 59)		Chief of Interpretation will prepare implementation plans and goals annually to allow time for proper implementation of the LRIP.		▮				

Research and Planning Documents continued

Project	PMIS #	Details	Total Cost	FY 2006	FY 2007	FY 2008	FY 2009	FY 2010 & beyond
Research Data for Effective Interpretation (page 60)		Conduct historical research and adapt findings for use by interpreters. Work with other preserve divisions to obtain information on natural and archeological research. Data will be incorporated into interpretive programs.	$40,000 for microfilm, reader, & travel	████	████	████	████	████
Research Available Media (page 60)		Research and plan a variety of media to respond to visitor questions concerning natural and cultural history.	Research cost will be incorporated into base funding.		████	████	████	████
Visitor Studies Profile (page 61)		Schedule and conduct visitor studies to develop profiles of visitor interests and expectations.	$25,000 based on Visitor Services Project			████	████	

Tallgrass Prairie National Preserve Long-Range Interpretive Plan

Sale Items

Project	PMIS #	Details	Total Cost	FY 2006	FY 2007	FY 2008	FY 2009	FY 2010 & beyond
Preserve Video (page 49)		Develop a video and DVD for sale to visitors on all the major experience opportunities available at the preserve with the preserve partner. Hire a firm to produce.	Collaborate with bookstore partner		�	�		
CD ROM of Images (page 49)		Develop a CD-ROM of images of the ranch and prairie for sale in the bookstore.	"	�	�			
Clothing Items (page 57)		Work with partner to develop clothing sale items displaying thematic messages.	"		�	▒	▒	
Preserve Patch (page 57)		Develop a preserve patch displaying the visual image of the preserve with input from partner.	"	▒				
Site Specific Books (page 58)		See Publications	"					
Audio Tour on CD Or Video Tour on DVD (pages 49 and 65)		Work with partner to develop an audio/video tour of the historic ranch on CD or DVD for sale.	"		▒	▒		

Tallgrass Prairie National Preserve Long-Range Interpretive Plan

Natural and Cultural Activities

Project	PMIS #	Details	Total Cost	FY 2006	FY 2007	FY 2008	FY 2009	FY 2010 & beyond
Reintroduction of Prairie and Crops for Interpretation (pages 74-75)	52732	Restore native vegetation and agricultural crops along Fox Creek bottomland area to reflect the historic landscape and to supplement interpretation of ranching and farming history. Include specific recommendations for farming culture in the bottomland cultural area such as orchards, gardens, and crops interpreted through the use of small trailside waysides and exhibits.	$500,000	Program development contingent upon funding.				
Develop Cultural Demonstrations and Activities Associated with Restored Prairie and Agriculture (page 75)		Agricultural crops reintroduced in the bottomland area will be used to interpret the agricultural practices through cultural farming and harvesting demonstrations. Activities associated with this reintroduced area include historic living history farming demonstrations, special events, scheduled guided walks, informal roving, and other activities.	$60,000 for demonstrator services, supplies, and equipment	Program dependent upon funding for development of area.				
Wildflower Program (page 76)		Develop a wildflower program with local scouts and 4-H groups in the bottomland trail area. Groups will assist in the construction of a limestone planter and then plant wildflowers appropriate to the area. Program will concentrate around learning new species, development of a brochure, and other activities to promote stewardship.	$3,000					

Tallgrass Prairie National Preserve Long-Range Interpretive Plan

Natural and Cultural Activities continued

Project	PMIS #	Details	Total Cost	FY 2006	FY 2007	FY 2008	FY 2009	FY 2010 & beyond
Backcountry Day Hiking Program (pages 77-78)		Non-motorized visitor access to the prairie by utilizing existing ranch roads. Hiking brochure and map, administrative supplies, and oversight will be required for this project.	$5,000 for supplies. See Publications	�largeshaded				
Develop New Trail to Bottomland Trail (page 75)		Foot trail will link the Bottomland Trail, visitor center, historic bottomland agricultural demonstration area, and ranch headquarters.	$250,000			▪shaded		▪shaded

Curatorial

Project	PMIS #	Details	Total Cost	FY 2006	FY 2007	FY 2008	FY 2009	FY 2010 & beyond
Photograph Objects (page 50)		Systematically photograph all objects at the preserve for documentation. Photographs will correspond to artifact inventory.	$8,000 salary & supplies	▮	▮			
Contract Agricultural Equipment Specialist (page 50)		Contract an agricultural equipment specialist to assess privately owned farm objects that are stored in the barn. Completion of the assessment will aid in the determination of which objects to acquire for museum storage, display, or for permanent exhibit.	$3,000	▮	▮			
Assess Artifacts in the Ranch House, School, and Outbuildings (page 50)		Assess all objects to determine their origins, provenance, period of manufacture, and condition. Goal is to determine whether to acquire these artifacts/objects as NPS property.	$5,000 travel & specialist services.	▮	▮			
Improve Storage of Historic Objects and Documents (pages 50 and 87)	38556	Upgrade storage materials and cabinets used to hold museum objects and documents.	$5,000	▮				
UV Film for Windows (page 50)		Place ultra violet film on all windows in the house, barn, and school to lower light levels and the direct sunlight's damaging effects on museum artifacts and objects.	$6,000	▮	▮			
Acquire Items and Artifacts for Display (page 50)		Acquire items based on the findings of the Scope of Collections statement for the preserve. Items should directly relate to the preserve for use in museum exhibits, programs, and collections.	$300,000			▮	▮	

Tallgrass Prairie National Preserve Long-Range Interpretive Plan

Visitor Center

Project	PMIS #	Details	Total Cost	FY 2006	FY 2007	FY 2008	FY 2009	FY 2010 & beyond
Construct Visitor Service Facilities (pages 83–89)	77288	Design and construct a visitor services complex to include a visitor center, maintenance facility, storage/shuttle building, outdoor amphitheater, shuttle road, entrance road, and parking area for 150 cars and 10 buses.	$11,454,000 for total facility			▓		
Outdoor Exhibits and Interpretive Space (page 85)		Provide basic orientation to visitors through the use of outdoor information kiosks and exhibits. Landscaped plaza will create both educational and reflective areas as another means of visitor experience.	$150,000 for outdoor exhibits			▓		
Theater with Audiovisual Program (page 86)		Develop a new 15 – 20 minute high definition video to showcase the five interpretive themes. Theater will be dedicated to audiovisual and formal presentations. AV program will be in several foreign languages.	$250,000			▓		
Develop a Visitor Center Museum Exhibit Proposal Plan (pages 87–88)		Develop a museum exhibit proposal, design, and production plan for the visitor center. The plan would detail exhibit descriptions, exhibit room layout and selection of media, artifacts, objects, and content.	$140,000			▓		

Visitor Center continued

Project	PMIS #	Details	Total Cost	FY 2006	FY 2007	FY 2008	FY 2009	FY 2010 & beyond
Produce and Install Museum Exhibits (pages 88–89)		Produce and install museum exhibits as described in the museum exhibit plan. Exhibits would integrate media to provide a good balance of interactive tactile, graphics, and audio/video. Museum exhibits adjacent to the lobby would incorporate all five interpretive themes.	$1,000,000					
Entrance Sign (page 63)		Plan, produce, and install a prominent and distinctive sign appropriate to the character of the preserve and leave no doubt that visitors are entering a National Park Service area.	$15,000					

Class C Cost Estimates from Visitor Center Site Alternative & EA, General Management Plan (12/2000) + 20%, and PMIS project statements in 2005 dollars

Tallgrass Prairie National Preserve Long-Range Interpretive Plan

STAFFING NEEDS

Chief of Interpretation and Visitor Services
GS-0025-12 (1 FTE)

Historian
GS-0170-09 (1 FTE)

Park Ranger (Lead)
GS-0025-05/07/09 (1 FTE)

Park Guide
GS-090-05 (2 FTE)

Cultural Demonstrator (Wrangler or Farmer)
GS-0025-07 (Subject to Furlough)

Cultural Demonstrator (Wrangler or Farmer)
GS-0025-05 (temp)

Park Ranger
GS-0025-05 (9 temp)

Park Guide
GS-0090-04 (5 temp, intermittent)

FUNDING

Suggestions for PMIS Proposals

Use bullets if possible. Cut and paste from a word document.

Set line spacing at 1 ½ if possible.

Use bold text to accentuate subtitles.

Where possible itemize costs.

Link project proposals to current initiatives. For example, link interpretive proposals to the Interpretive Development Program.

Define terms that may not be understood by everyone.

Sources

Annual Operating Funds or Park Base – Fund Type 01

This is the primary source of recurring operational funding used for park management, interpretation, visitor services, maintenance, and resource protection. Parks request base increases through the Operations Formulation System (OFS).

Challenge Cost-Share – Fund Type 01

The program provides a maximum of 50% cost-share grant to expedite mutually beneficial projects with outside sources. The program increases awareness and participation by the public in the preservation and improvement of National Park Service recreational, cultural, and natural resources. Park partners may include individuals, groups, companies, corporation, state and local agencies and other non-Federal entities that donate funds, equipment, supplies or labor to complete a park project. Projects are intended to be small, able to be completed in one year, and consistent with planning documents.

Cultural Cyclic Maintenance – Fund Type 01

Funds are used for the maintenance and rehabilitation of historic structures and museum collections. Appropriate projects include predictable tasks performed on a fixed periodic basis with a cycle longer than one year. The work may be completed through contracts or seasonal day labor.

Donations - Fund Type 26

Parks are authorized to accept and use donated funds to meet the purposes of the National Park Service. Use of these funds is strictly controlled, must be consistent with legislative authority, and must meet with the approval of the grantor.

Emergency Relief and Storm Damage – Fund Type 04

Funding may be available for emergency repairs to park facilities damaged by acts of nature and structural fire. Requests for funding should be submitted to the Regional Office for review and approval.

Exhibit Rehab and Preservation Program – Fund Type 01

The Major Rehab Program administered by Harpers Ferry Center (HFC) provides repair, rehabilitation or replacement of audiovisuals and exhibits, preservation of artifacts and museum specimens, and acquisition of historic furnishings. Interpretive media projects in newly authorized areas may also be submitted.

Fee Program – Fund Type 04

These no-year funds offset park base funding. They allow flexibility to carry base funding across fiscal years, but only on a very limited basis.

Fee Demonstration Program – Fund Type 25

The recreation fee demonstration program allows parks that collect fees to retain 80% of the revenues generated. The remaining 20 percent will be made available service-wide.

Information Publications Program – Fund Type 01

Park folders, handbooks, posters, and other publications prepared by Harpers Ferry Center for parks are funded from this account. Note: Regional offices frequently supplement funding for folders.

National Parks Pass – Fund Type 22

Seventy percent of proceeds from Pass sales remain with the selling park to fund approved projects. The remaining proceeds support projects service-wide.

Parks as Classrooms – Fund Type 01

Funds may be requested to promote cooperative education programs combining park settings and classroom study. Eligible activities include those presented at the park, at schools and community organizations.

Park Concessions Franchise Fees – Fund Type 99

Eighty percent of concessions franchise fees generated at a park are available to that park for approved projects (concessions related needs, environmental and energy efficiency projects, visitor services, resource management programs). The remaining 20 percent will be made available for service-wide projects.

Regular Cyclic Maintenance – Fund Type 01

To qualify for funding projects must be submitted to the park's ten-year cyclic maintenance program. Funds may be used to maintain park roads, trails, building, utility systems, and other facilities. Appropriate projects include tasks recurring on a fixed periodic cycle that is longer than one year and no longer than ten years. Some Regions also fund Exhibit Cyclic Maintenance and Natural Resources Cyclic Maintenance from this fund source.

Repair and Rehabilitation – Fund Type 01

Funding is used to cover the cost of repair and rehabilitation of existing facilities, roads, trails and utility systems. Permanent employee's salaries should not be charged to repair and rehabilitation accounts.

Volunteers-in-Parks (VIP) – Fund Type 01

Funding may be requested for training and incidental expenses such as uniforms, period clothing, local travel, supplies, lodging, meals and other direct costs chargeable to the Volunteer-in-Parks Program.

MEDIA DESIGN AND PRODUCTION

There are many options for parks that want to accomplish media projects. Harpers Ferry Center staff, park staff, contractors and others can do the work; development processes vary with the source of media development assistance. Other project considerations include value analysis, Development Advisory Board review, government contracting procedures, and the need for partner collaboration. Park staff should collaborate with media specialists in developing an effective and efficient strategy.

Strategies for Developing Media Projects

Who Will Do the Work?

Major tasks for team members include project management, review, research, planning, design, contracting, detailing, fabrication and evaluation. Team members can be assembled from several sources. Park staff may have expertise to lead or participate in project development.

Harpers Ferry Center can develop projects in-house or through contractors or help parks task assist programs or the Interpretive Media Institute. Parks may locate contractors through a request for proposal, Harpers Ferry Center general indefinite quantity contractor lists, or a park indefinite quantity list. Other sources of possible assistance include subcontractors, architectural firms, partners, cooperating associations, friends groups, park volunteers, support offices, clusters, neighbor parks, regional offices and service centers.

How Will They Do It?

Development processes vary, and tend to be linked to team preferences. Harpers Ferry Center processes start with the Long-Range Interpretive Plan for guidance and proceeds through Schematic Design, Concept Design, Final Design, and Fabrication. Contractors typically follow a process including Master Plan, Schematic Design, Concept Design, and Fabrication. Architectural firms may follow Concept Design with Schematic Design, Construction Documents, and Construction. Curators, Smithsonian, American Association of Museums and others can suggest additional processes.

How Long Will It Take?

Schedules vary according to project conditions and team member availability. A normal process could include two years, one year for planning and design and a second year for production. Accelerated projects, not usually practical, may only take six months for planning and design and six months for production. A more extended project could require five years, 3.5 for planning and design and 1.5 to produce. Funding and facility development problems may delay either schedule.

How Much Will It Cost?

Project cost can vary. Determinates include available money, estimated cost, who controls the budget, and what controls are used.

What Resources Does the Park Have?

Survey park staff to identify specialized skills for media work. Identify graphics, film footage, artifacts, specimens, exhibit spaces, facilities, and other infrastructure that can contribute to a successful project.

Keys to Successful Media Projects

Launching a Media Project

Recognize the importance of media in the park's overall program for visitors.

Insure that interpretive themes and objectives are defined before media planning.

Honor plans that have been approved – Long-Range Interpretive Plans, General Management Plans, media plans.

Insure that project goals are clearly laid out in advance.

Involve media specialists in facility design from the beginning.

Make comments on media concepts, techniques, and solutions early in the process.

Recognize the level of effort required on the part of park staff, and plan accordingly.

Invite park staff with needed knowledge, skills, and abilities to participate in planning.

Assign a project manager for the park with authority to make decisions.

Planning, Designing, and Producing the Project

Take time to prepare and use effective contracts and project agreements.

Allow the project team to exercise creativity - don't provide the solution up front.

Manage the budget in a clear and efficient way for the project team; don't let funding lapses or glitches stall the project.

Provide timely and constructive reviews of project submittals.

Insure that project requirements, policies and standards are met; consider universal design, object conservation, diverse audiences, and sustainability.

Work with partners and other stakeholders to promote teamwork, and to resolve potential problems and conflicts.

Systematically evaluate effectiveness of media throughout the process.

Take ownership of the project before, during, and after completion.

EVALUATION

Introduction

Evaluation is an essential part of planning and operating a park interpretive program. Over the years it has become increasingly evident that interpretation facilities, media and activities benefit from evaluation. Evaluation should begin during planning and development of interpretive program components. A variety of evaluation activities tailored to specific tasks and questions to be answered should be an ongoing process following program implementation.

A complete evaluation program should include three cycles.

FRONT-END EVALUATIONS are appropriate when conceptual planning considers themes, story lines and program ideas.

FORMATIVE EVALUATIONS are done during a process, such as early fabrication of exhibits and test run of activities. Formative evaluations are increasing in the Park Service, especially with the implementation of GPRA and value analysis.

SUMMATIVE OR REMEDIAL EVALUATIONS are performed at the end of a process. Summative evaluations have been more common in government agencies. Performance is measured and assessed at the end of a fiscal year. Achievement of media objectives is determined after the media are installed for a period of time. Achievement of short-term educational goals is measured at the conclusion of a program.

National Park Service Evaluation Program

VISITOR SERVICES PROJECT assesses visitor backgrounds, preferences, activities, and opinions through surveys. The Cooperative Park Study Unit (CPSU) at the University of Idaho coordinates the program.

GOVERNMENT PERFORMANCE AND RESULTS ACT (GPRA) holds offices and parks accountable for defining and assessing desired outcomes. Park staff conducts evaluation of goal accomplishment annually.

VALUE ANALYSIS PROGRAM assesses the cost effectiveness of design and construction projects in excess of $500,000.

POST OCCUPANCY EVALUATION PROGRAM (POE) assesses the effectiveness of interpretive facilities and media. The program is coordinated by Denver Service Center and Harpers Ferry Center and may be applied following implementation of media proposals.

POST CONSTRUCTION EVALUATION coordinated by Denver Service Center looks at the quality of construction of facilities built by DSC.

PARK INITIATED EVALUATIONS are conducted or contracted by parks with assistance from regional offices, service centers and the Washington Office of Interpretation and Visitor Services.

Techniques

The following techniques are recommended for consideration as PARK INITIATED EVALUATIONS for implementation at Tallgrass Prairie National Preserve.

This is not intended as an all-inclusive list. These methods were selected because they can be applied with relative ease and because they represent techniques with low to moderate cost and time commitments that yield moderate to high value/benefits. A Field Guide for Evaluating National Park Service Interpretation by Brett Wright and Marcella Wells provides a complete description of these and other techniques.

Front End Evaluations

Recorded observation and dry runs are appropriate at the preserve to determine that each component of interpretive and education program is meeting the needs of visitors and park management. Simple dry runs in the barn and ranch house when preparing for future development can analyze exhibit concepts before investing in permanent exhibit production and installation.

Importance/Performance Analysis

Cost - Low   Time - Moderate   Value – High

This analysis, more quantitative than qualitative, is an empirical test used to obtain assessment of visitor satisfaction. The analysis helps determine which areas of a program require the most resources and attention, which resources could be reduced or eliminated from particular areas of a program, or which efforts should be maintained. This technique is easily understood, easily displayed, easily interpreted to obtain data that can be applied readily to program decisions. It can be used to evaluate both overall program as well as single activities.

Auditing

Cost – Moderate   Time - Moderate   Value - Moderate/High

Auditing helps supervisors guide development of interpretive activities and interpreters improve their performance. The auditor and interpreter set and discuss objectives prior to the audit. The auditor then conducts the formal audit using checklists adapted to the program being audited. A post-audit conference, a direct two-way communication, must take place as soon as possible after the formal audit. It provides prompt feedback to the interpreter being audited and provide basis for follow-up coaching. The evaluator is able to assess interpreter's actual performance in terms of content and technique. Coaching aspects of the audit to lessen the intimidation of the evaluation process and provide the opportunity to correct inconsistencies before they become habit.

Interviewing

Cost - Low/Moderate   Time - High   Value – High

There are three approaches to interviewing. In each a single interviewer facilitates the conversation to gather data that reveals the interviewees perspective by allowing them to express their understanding of a situation in their own words. The Informal Conversational Interview, or unstructured interview, presents open-ended questions in spontaneous, free-flowing conversation. The Interview Guide Approach, or semi-structured interview, uses predetermined questions or issues, but the interviewer adapts wording and sequence flexibly during the interview. This approach may be used effectively for group interviews where the facilitator focuses the conversation. The Standardized Open Ended Interview presents the same carefully worded questions in the same sequence to all interviewees. This method reduces interviewer bias and makes data analysis easier than other methods. Regardless of the approach to interviewing, response rates for interviews are usually higher than with a questionnaire and more complex issues can be addressed.

Focus Groups

Cost - Low   Time - Moderate   Value – High

Focus groups are small groups formed specifically to discuss a particular question, concern or problem and led by a well-trained discussion leader who uses a study guide to facilitate the topic of discussion. Focus groups are helpful as formative and summative evaluations. They capitalize on the value of group dynamics to assure high level of validity while examining issues and concerns in a social context. This technique yields qualitative information often missed in statistical studies. It can be used to evaluate the message transmitted, determine visitor perceptions, measure strengths and weaknesses, or anticipate visitor needs for both personal and non-personal interpretation. Focus Groups: A Tool for Evaluating Interpretive Services, a National Park Service training package, describes procedures for conducting focus group evaluations.

Observation

Cost - Low   Time - Moderate/High   Value - Moderate/High

This qualitative technique can effectively evaluate interpretive episodes as they occur. Observing people in a natural setting can reveal high quality information not revealed by more quantitative techniques. Observational data helps understand the impacts of interpretive programs without encumbering visitors. It can be applied to interpretation in a variety of overt and covert observation strategies (direct, indirect, unobtrusive, and interactive) to gather observational data. The evaluator might observe Statistical Evidence such as program attendance and other visitor use data. Physical Evidence of tile and carpet wear around exhibits, trail wear and wear on exhibit material can expose visitor interests and desires. Archival Evidence includes permits, sales records, number of complaints and compliments and trail logs. Participant Observation of non-participation, time dedicated to a particular activity, body language and language and conversation reveals interests. Contrived Observation techniques use video, audio tape, or time-lapse photography.

Connoisseurship and Criticism

Cost - Moderate   Time - Low/Moderate   Value – Moderate

The strength of this technique lies in its capability to turn trained observation into statements about interpretive quality through interpretation and evaluation of what is observed. This qualitative method yields valuable information about content, quality, and presentation of interpretive activities. An evaluator with training, experience and refined perceptual capabilities conducts the evaluation and prepares a critical narrative to help interpreters see, understand and appraise situations being critiqued. The written critique includes three components. A descriptive section presents a vivid and factual description of the situation. An interpretive section accounts for the interactions perceived in the situation by interpreting processes observed. The evaluator presents value judgments based on criteria related to the specific situation and the needs of the creator or presenter of the interpretive experience.

APPENDICES

APPENDIX 1 - PLANNING TEAM AND CONSULTANTS

Tallgrass Prairie National Preserve

Steve Miller	Superintendent
Heather Brown	Chief of Interpretation
Anne-Marie Rizzi	Administrative Officer
Paula Andersen	Natural Resource Manager
Louise Carlin	Kansas Park Trust
Bob King	Facility Manager

Midwest Archeological Center

Bruce Jones	Archeologist

Harpers Ferry Center

Sarah Heald	Historic Furnishings
Dave McLean	Museum Exhibits
Keith Morgan	Park Ranger – Planner (Team Leader)
Elizabeth Kerwin-Nisbet	Wayside Exhibits
Richard Devries	Publications

APPENDIX 2 - VISITOR QUESTIONS

General

Why is the tallgrass prairie one of the most endangered ecosystems in the world?

Geology

- What caused these rolling hills? Most of Kansas appears flat.
- What geologic forces wrought the landscape to the shape it is today?
- Why doesn't the grass grow as high on the hills?
- Why do I see oil wells on my ride into the park?
- What type of rock is flint? Why is it here?

Biology

- What is the difference between Switch, Indian and Bluestem grasses?
- Do different animals live in the different grasses?
- How is the tallgrass different from the grass in my lawn? Why should I care that very little of it survives?
- What adaptations help native animals survive in the tallgrass?
- What exotic species of animals have been introduced? How have they impacted the land?
- What lives in the waters and riparian communities?
- How do migratory and resident birds use the tallgrass prairie?
- Are there any unique micro-organisms floating around?
- What are the different impacts of cattle and bison on the prairie?
- Tell me more about the "prairie underground"? What examples of biological diversity (plants, animals) do we see in the prairie? Why is biological diversity important to ecosystem survival?

Endless Sky Country

- How clean is the air?
- How much light pollution is evident at night?

- Why is it so windy here under the endless sky?
- How does weather in other parts of the country affect the weather at the preserve?

History

- The Jones and Williams families arrive on the scene not long after the civil war. They were originally from the South. Did their move tie into the war at all?
- Were there bad feelings toward either family?
- How does Williams' story tie into the larger story of social change after the civil war?
- How does that family's story play into the history of Kansas and the history of other African-American settlements?
- Why didn't they choose to move to Nicodemus with other free men and women? Were they part of the great "exodust"?
- Does the Williams' story tie into the story of the Dunlap settlement north of the preserve?

APPENDIX 3 - VISITOR CENTER PLANNING SPECIFICATIONS

Parking Lots

- How many spaces are there for cars, busses, and special vehicles?
- Wheelchair accessible.
- Good relationship (distance, grade) of lot to building.
- Visibility of building from parking spaces.
- Accommodation of mass transportation vehicle's path through parking lot leaving or arriving from trips to the preserve.
- Shelter from weather for visitors waiting for mass transportation vehicles.

Access To and From Visitor Center

- Ease of grade for visitors using wheel chairs.
- Retaining rails where needed.
- Good separation of the building's landscape initial plantings from visitor pathways so as not to become impedance when they mature.
- Obvious location of building's entrance so as not to confuse visitors.
- Power assisted doors to facilitate both visitors and employees that are using wheel chairs.
- Prominently marked exit doors from building.
- Outside paving texture of a nature so as not to be a hindrance to easy rolling of wheel chairs, yet not so smooth as to be slippery when wet or icy.
- Arrival tread devices just inside front door designed to remove shoe borne debris from outdoors.
- Indoor carpets of a color and visual texture so as to match outdoor dirt and debris.

Reception

- If possible locate rest rooms prominently signed just outside of front entrance. This will greatly reduce the number of arriving visitors who ask for restrooms, going back out the front door, using facilities, and then entering the front door a second time. Additionally it will totally eliminate one more question that the front desk attendant has to answer. Restrooms outside the visitor center can be left open for after hour visitors. Malfunctioning restrooms that are outside the visitor center can not disrupt inside activities with foul smells or overflowing sewage water. Repair of restrooms is less disrupting when the facilities are outside. Employee restrooms should be provided inside the building. This will assist employee surveillance of building.

- Locate reception desk so it is obvious to incoming visitors and an active agent in the control of visitors coming and going. Locate employee office adjoining front desk so if necessary one person can function as receptionist and accomplish other work when visitation is low. The door to this office should open near the front desk but have a baffle wall within the support office that hides office clutter from view by visitors. If possible provide a viewing slit (6 inches high x 2ft long) so employees seated behind the wall can see into the lobby area. The reception desk should have a high (stand up) section and a lower height for wheelchair confined visitors. The cash register (if only one) should be placed at the lower level so it is accessible to a wheel chaired employee. The end of the desk that accommodates the wheel chair should be cantilevered so as not to restrict the movement of the wheel chair person's legs when maneuvering around the end. Provide lighting, power and audiovisual controls to this desk to allow operation of the entire visitor use area by one employee. Provide two pin-up surface areas in close proximity to this desk, one behind the desk so only the employee can alter it and one perpendicular to both the visitor and the employee so both can touch. This technique often serves more than the one person to which the employee is speaking.

Lobby

- Besides the reception desk, the lobby is to be the decision point for the visitor. To best facilitate flow to the various attractions offered within the visitor center, the lobby should function as the hub from which one leaves and returns after the choice of each attraction. The probable attractions are audiovisual room, exhibit room, bookstore, trip planning area, adjacent self-guided walks, transportation to historic ranch headquarters, and of course exit back out the front door.

Audiovisual Room

- This space should be close to the lobby and constructed to dampen sound spill from its program and not be affected by the noise or light from the lobby. Architectural equipment such as heating, ventilation, and air conditioning (HVAC) should not be located above or next to this space. There should be no windows in the theater. Emergency exits should be placed at the opposite end of the room from the door through which the visitor entered. All exits should have a lighted sign on a back-up power system. There should be an acoustic study executed to dampen the reverberating sound in the space. If the room is to be used for multiple uses it should have a level floor with moveable seating that is capable of stacking and storing. A separate dedicated room should be built for the storage of these chairs. If the room is to be maximized for a theater the floor should be sloped with fixed seating. This puts more restraints on location of seating for disabled visitors. Additionally this definitely sets the number of seats and requires answering questions of how many visitors are expected at one time, how crowds will be divided, and various other considerations. Electrical and audio-visual needs at the front of the theater where someone might want to give a program should be taken into consideration. Additionally there should be a count-down clock placed conspicuously outside the theater for visitors to know when the next show will begin. Public address systems blaring over the entire facility for this purpose are a more undesirable alternative.

Exhibit Room

- This room should be adjacent to the lobby with some separation to prevent sound spill from that noisy space. There should be no windows in the exhibit room. This eliminates competing with the wide fluctuations of light produced by the sun. The space should have at least a ten foot high ceiling into which is set a power grid-8 foot on center, beginning 4 feet out from the wall. Each of these power sources should be capable of handling 10-75 watt bulbs. The perimeter of the room should have under carpet wiring receptacles (18" off floor) concealed in the walls at a distance of eight feet apart. These power sources should each lead back to its own dedicated breaker at the main switch in the building. The floor should be smooth concrete or other material over which will be laid, carpet tiles which are not glued down. To power exhibits in the center of the room flat wiring will pass under these carpet tiles from receptacles around the edge of the room. With this capability built into the room that is to be populated with exhibits, future limitations are greatly reduced. Additionally, the architects, armed with this knowledge, can determine what kind of electrical loads are required and the effects it will have on the HVAC systems. Besides lights dedicated to exhibits, there should be a separate set of lights powered by a different circuit for illumination when cleaning up the place. These lights are just to be used for maintenance and not left on when exhibit lighting is on. Breaker boxes controlling all these lights should be secured in a place away from the public.

- It is good practice to have architects lay in proposed exhibit spaces 3/4 inch thick, 4ft x 8ft. (vertical) plywood sheets on all the wall studs starting one foot off the floor before sheathing the room with gypsum wall board. This provides a strong surface to which exhibit panels can be attached. When the space is reconfigured and new exhibits are hung, the old holes in the gypsum walls are spackled, sanded and repainted and the supporting plywood is as strong as ever.

APPENDIX 4 - EXHIBIT CONCEPTS

The following drawings present ideas for immediate and future exhibit
development at Tall Grass Prairie National Preserve.

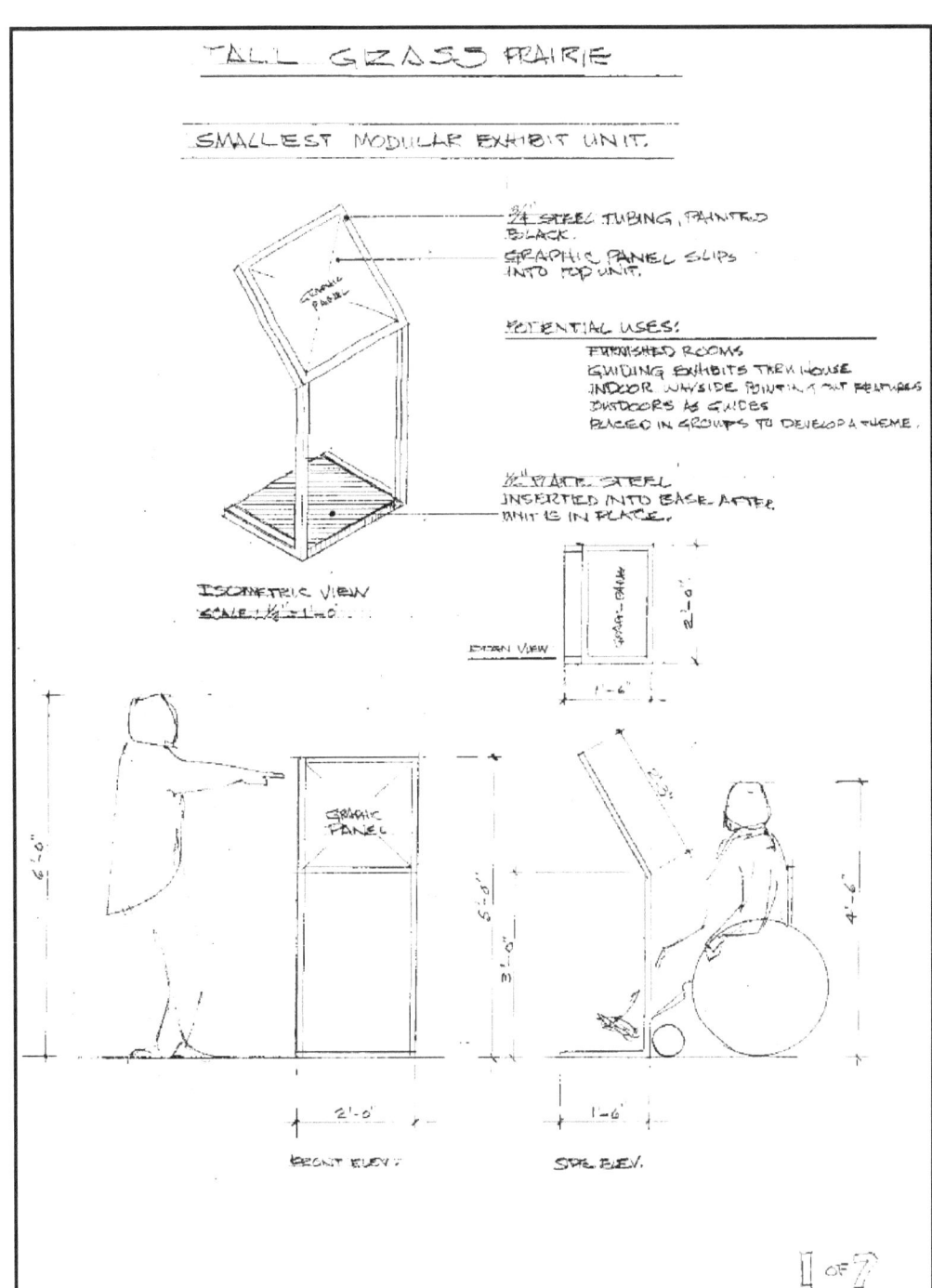

TALL GRASS PRAIRIE

SMALLEST MODULAR EXHIBIT UNIT.

3/4" STEEL TUBING, PAINTED BLACK.

GRAPHIC PANEL SLIPS INTO TOP UNIT.

POTENTIAL USES:

FURNISHED ROOMS
GUIDING EXHIBITS THRU HOUSE
INDOOR WAYSIDE POINTING OUT FEATURES
OUTDOORS AS GUIDES
PLACED IN GROUPS TO DEVELOP A THEME.

1/2" PLATE STEEL INSERTED INTO BASE AFTER UNIT IS IN PLACE.

ISOMETRIC VIEW
SCALE: 1/2" = 1'-0"

PLAN VIEW

GRAPHIC PANEL

FRONT ELEV.

SIDE ELEV.

1 of 7

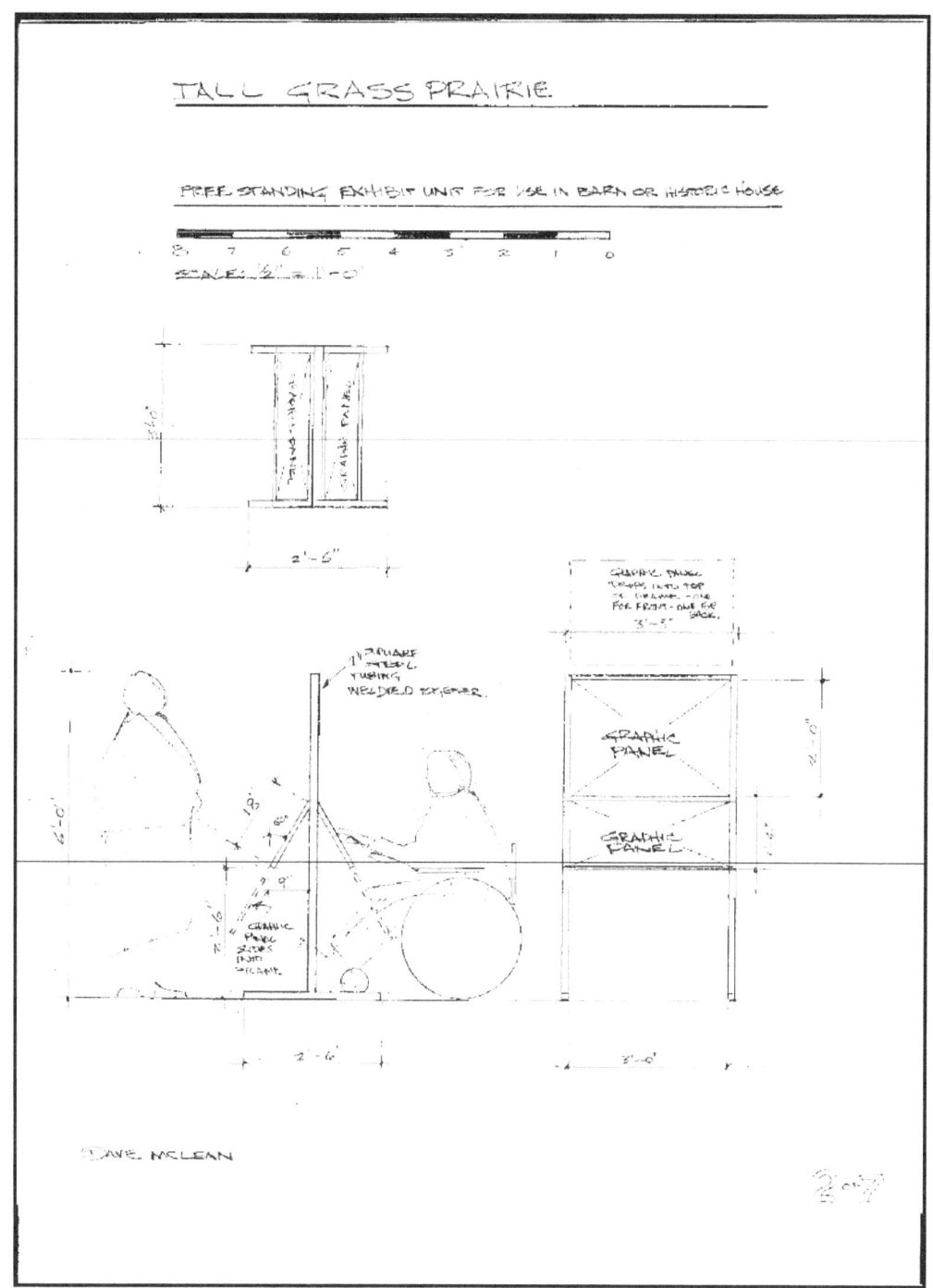

TALL GRASS PRAIRIE.

FREE STANDING EXHIBIT UNIT FOR USE IN BARN OR HISTORIC HOUSE

SCALE: ½" = 1'-0"

DAVE MCLEAN

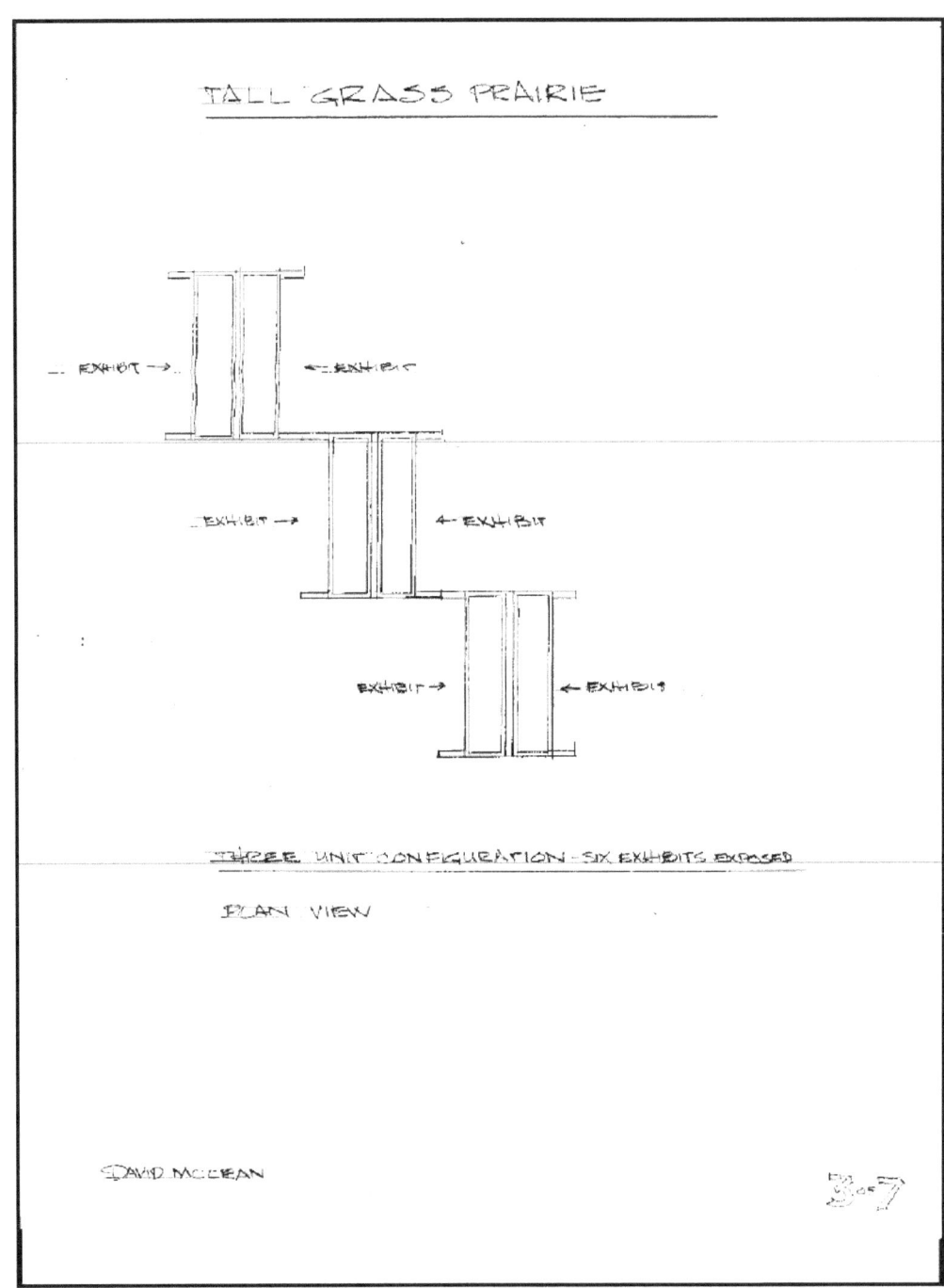

TALL GRASS PRAIRIE

THREE UNIT CONFIGURATION - SIX EXHIBITS EXPOSED

PLAN VIEW

DAVID McLEAN

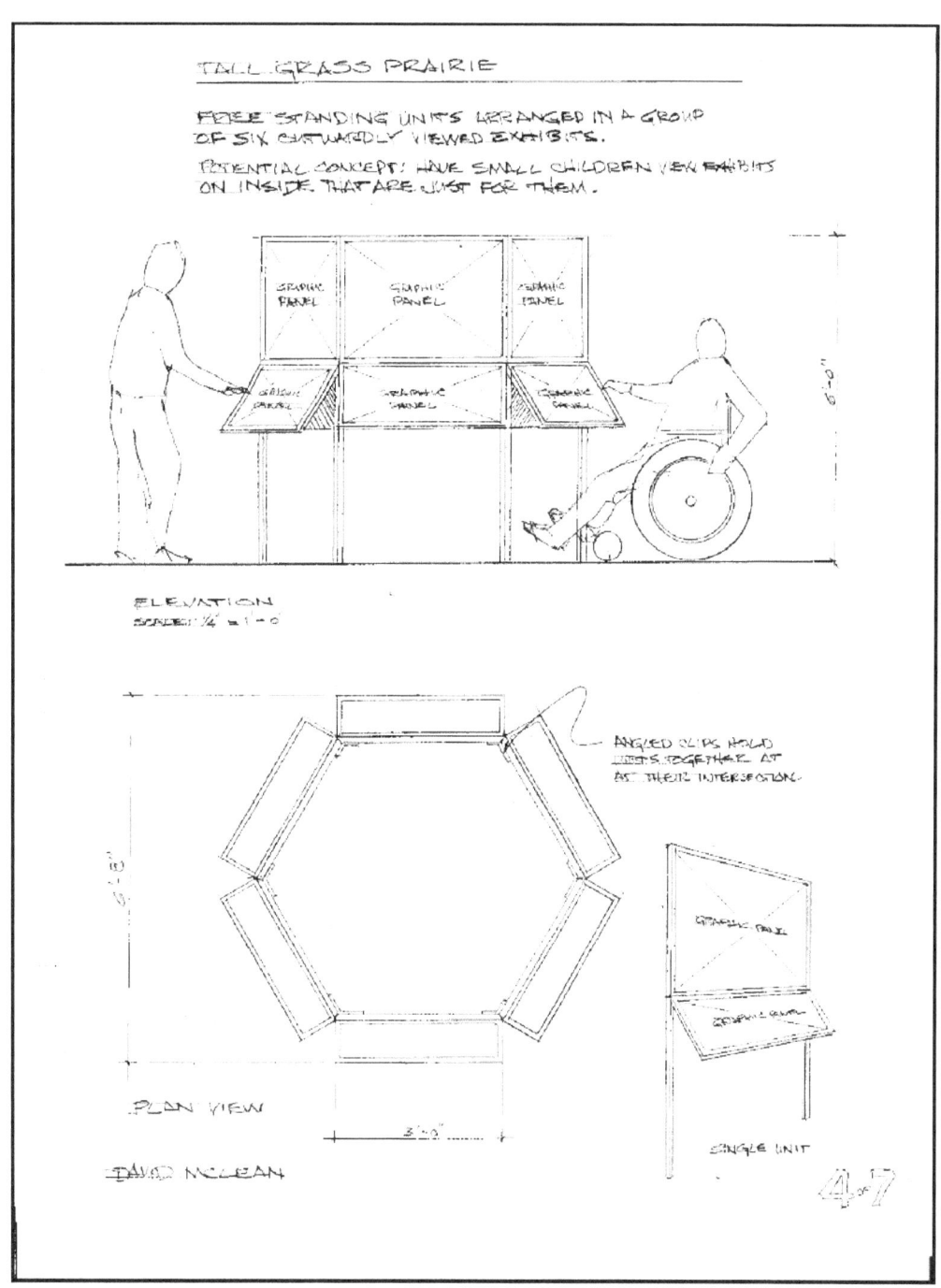

TALL GRASS PRAIRIE

FREE STANDING UNITS ARRANGED IN A GROUP OF SIX OUTWARDLY VIEWED EXHIBITS.

POTENTIAL CONCEPT: HAVE SMALL CHILDREN VIEW EXHIBITS ON INSIDE THAT ARE JUST FOR THEM.

GRAPHIC PANEL

ELEVATION
SCALE: 1/4" = 1'-0"

ANGLED CLIPS HOLD UNITS TOGETHER AT AT THEIR INTERSECTION.

GRAPHIC PANEL

PLAN VIEW

SINGLE UNIT

DAVID MCLEAN

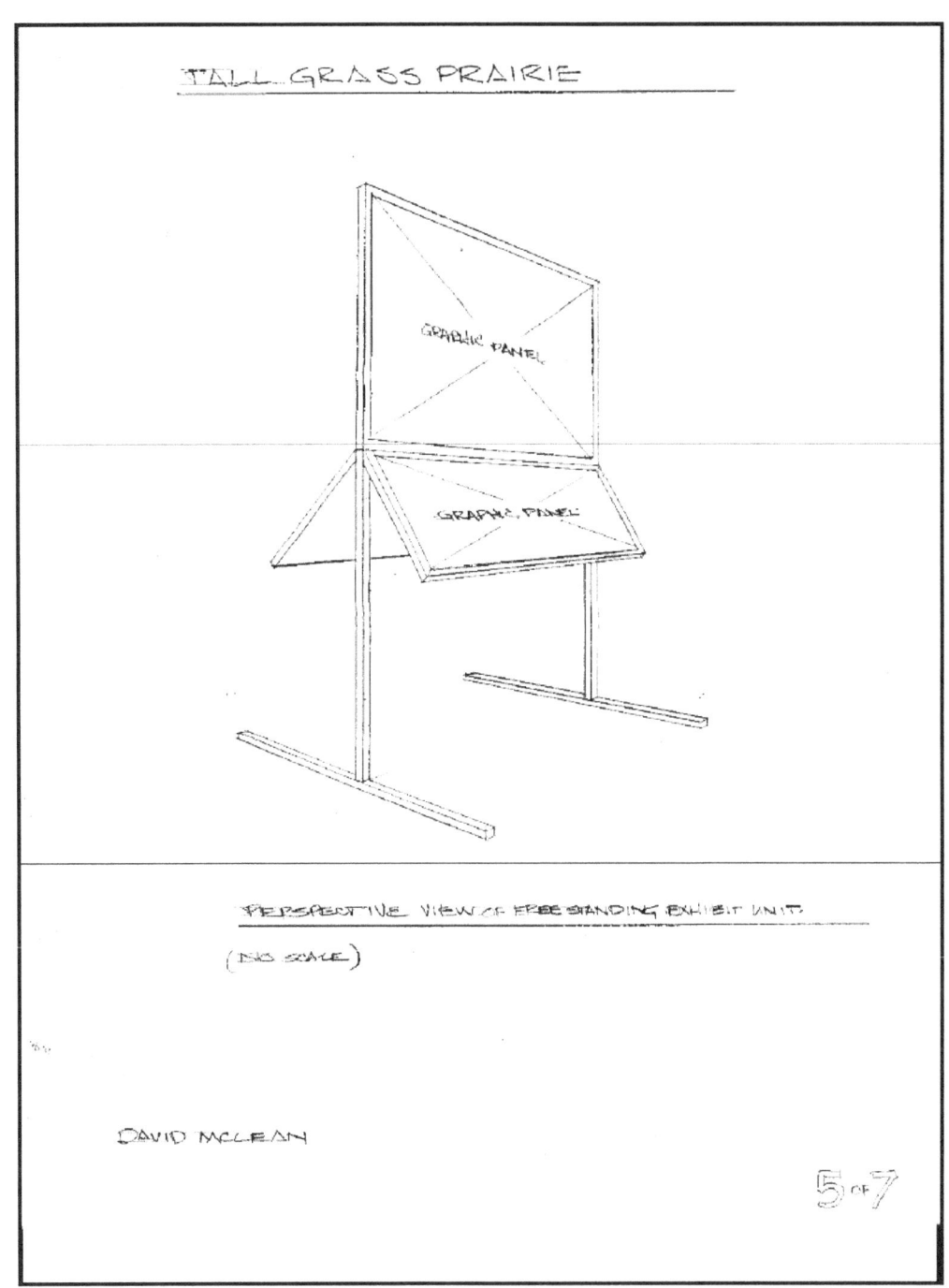

TALL GRASS PRAIRIE

GRAPHIC PANEL

GRAPHIC PANEL

PERSPECTIVE VIEW OF FREE STANDING EXHIBIT UNIT

(NO SCALE)

DAVID McCLEAN

5 of 7

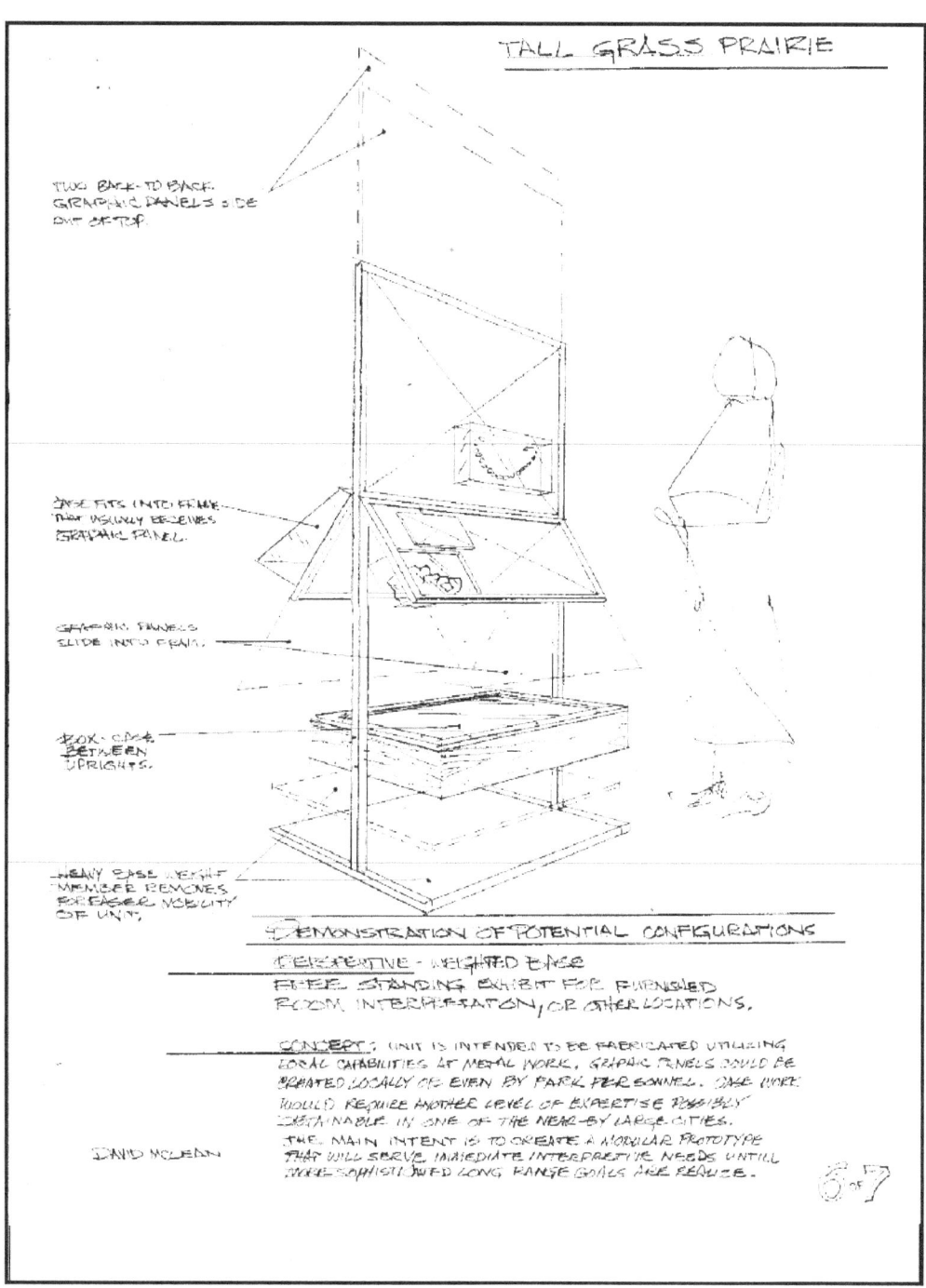

TWO BACK-TO-BACK
GRAPHIC PANELS SIDE
ONE SET-TOP.

CASE FITS INTO FRAME
THAT USUALLY RECEIVES
GRAPHIC PANEL.

GRAPHIC PANELS
SLIDE INTO FRAME.

BOX-CASE
BETWEEN
UPRIGHTS.

HEAVY BASE WEIGHT
MEMBER REMOVES
FOR EASER MOBILITY
OF UNIT.

DEMONSTRATION OF POTENTIAL CONFIGURATIONS

PERSPECTIVE - WEIGHTED BASE

FREE STANDING EXHIBIT FOR FURNISHED
ROOM INTERPRETATION, OR OTHER LOCATIONS.

CONCEPT: UNIT IS INTENDED TO BE FABRICATED UTILIZING
LOCAL CAPABILITIES AT METAL WORK. GRAPHIC PANELS COULD BE
CREATED LOCALLY OR EVEN BY PARK PERSONNEL. CASE WORK
WOULD REQUIRE ANOTHER LEVEL OF EXPERTISE POSSIBLY
OBTAINABLE IN ONE OF THE NEAR-BY LARGE CITIES.
THE MAIN INTENT IS TO CREATE A MODULAR PROTOTYPE
THAT WILL SERVE IMMEDIATE INTERPRETIVE NEEDS UNTILL
MORE SOPHISTICATED LONG RANGE GOALS ARE REALIZED.

DAVID MCLEAN

6 OF 7

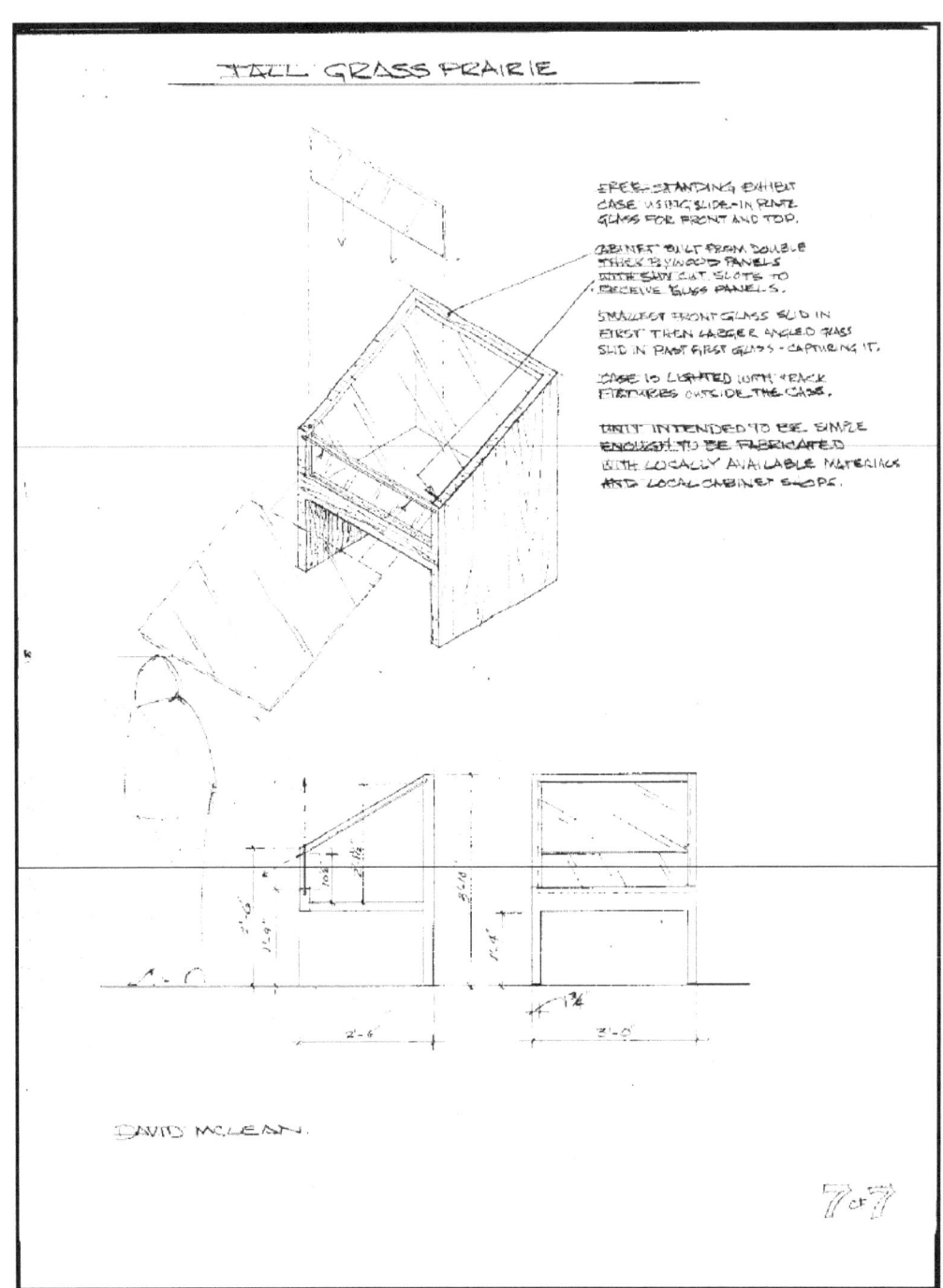

TALL GRASS PRAIRIE

FREE-STANDING EXHIBIT
CASE USING SLIDE-IN PLATE
GLASS FOR FRONT AND TOP.

CABINET BUILT FROM DOUBLE
THICK PLYWOOD PANELS
WITH SAW CUT SLOTS TO
RECEIVE GLASS PANELS.

SMALLEST FRONT GLASS SLID IN
FIRST THEN LARGER ANGLED GLASS
SLID IN PAST FIRST GLASS - CAPTURING IT.

CASE IS LIGHTED WITH TRACK
FIXTURES OUTSIDE THE CASE.

UNIT INTENDED TO BE SIMPLE
ENOUGH TO BE FABRICATED
WITH LOCALLY AVAILABLE MATERIALS
AND LOCAL CABINET SHOPS.

DAVID McLEAN.

7 of 7

APPENDIX 5 – FLOOR PLANS

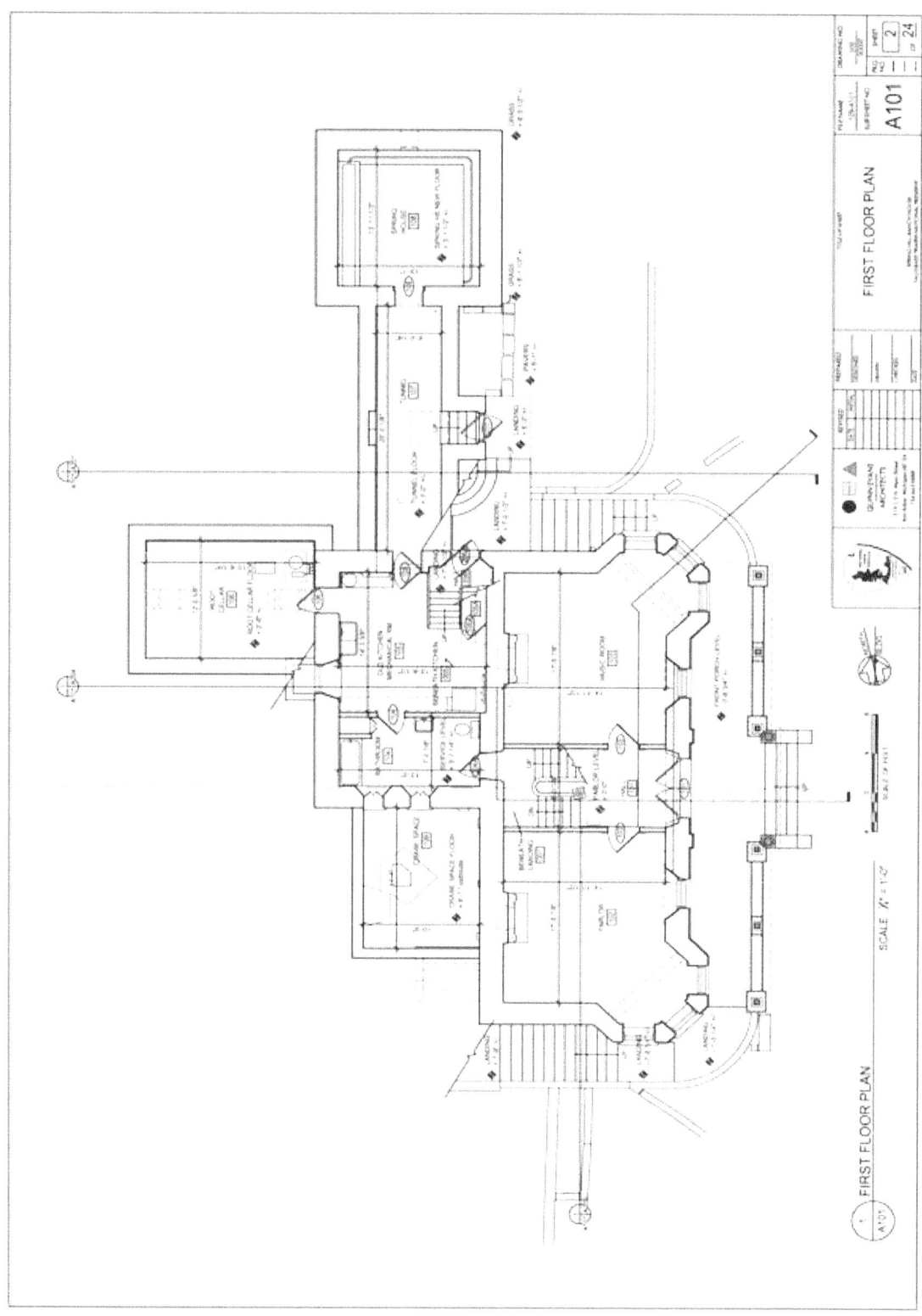

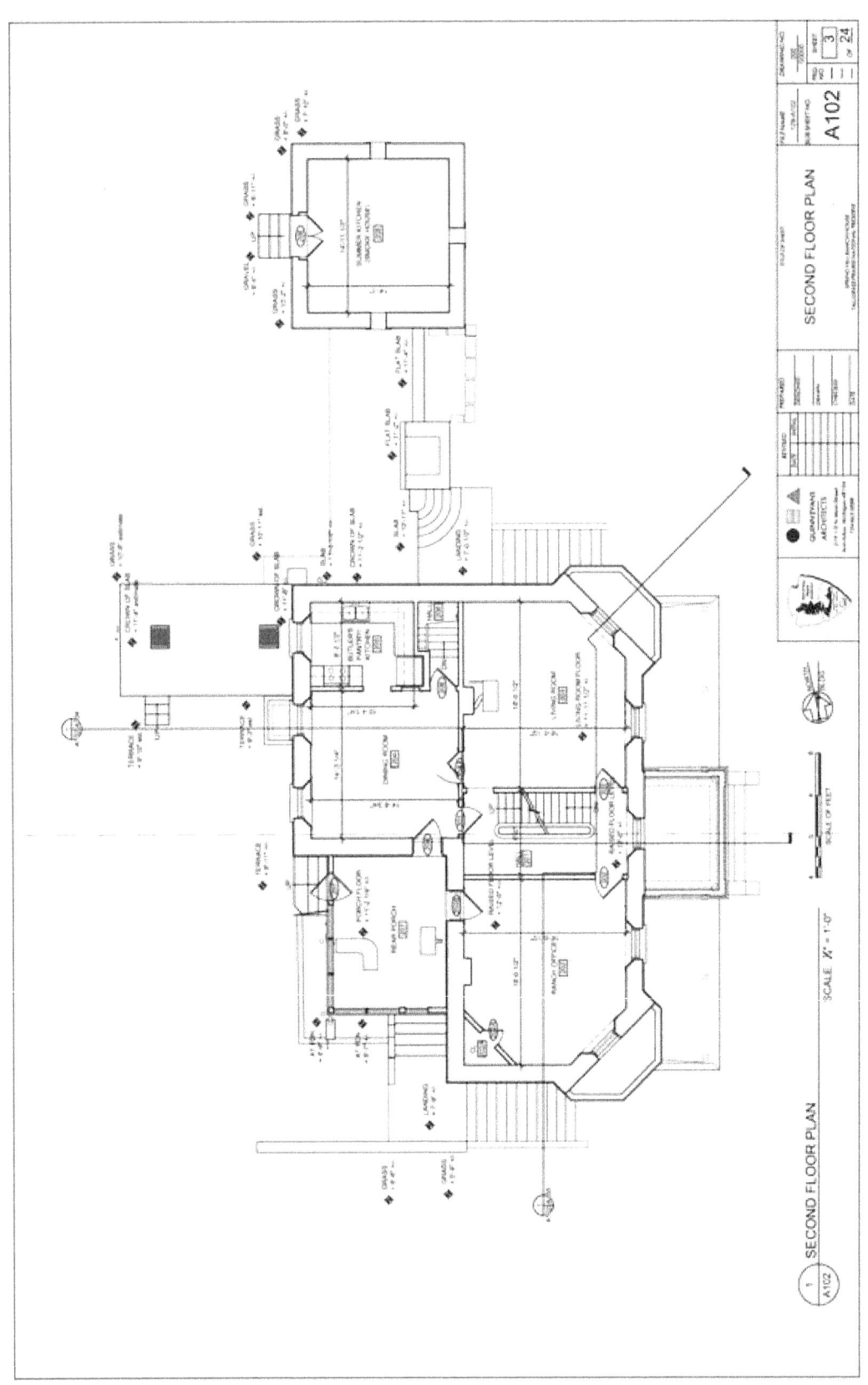

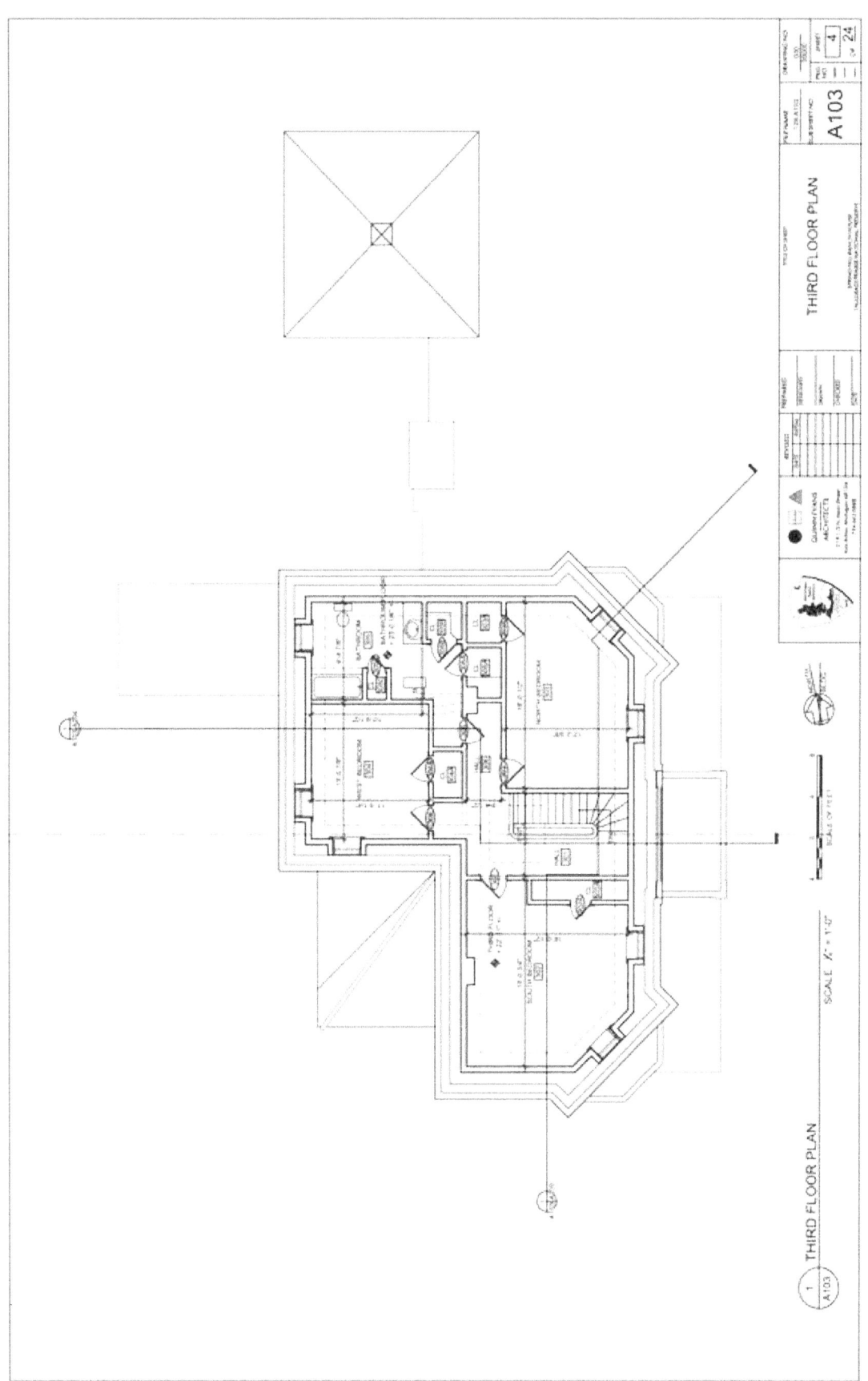

APPENDIX 6 - BIBLIOGRAPHY

<u>History and Prehistory in the National Park System and the National Historic Landmarks Program</u>, History Division, National Park Service, Washington, D. C., 1987.

<u>Natural History in the National Park System and on the National Registry of Natural Landmarks</u>, Natural Resource Report, National Park Service, Washington, D. C., 1990.

<u>Revision of the National Park Service's Thematic Framework</u>, National Park Service, Washington, D. C., 1996.

<u>General Management Plan – Tallgrass Prairie National Preserve</u>, National Park Service, Washington, D. C., 2000.

<u>Comprehensive Interpretive Planning, Interpretation and Education Guideline</u>, National Park Service, Washington, D.C., 2000.